"ROBBO"

- Unsung Hero

**THE BIOGRAPHY
OF PAUL ROBINSON**

First published 2015 by DB Publishing, an imprint of JMD Media Ltd, Nottingham, United Kingdom.

ISBN 9781780914541

"ROBBO"

- Unsung Hero

THE BIOGRAPHY
OF PAUL ROBINSON

Paul Robinson with Keith Dixon

Contents

Introduction

by Keith Dixon

ROBBO – UNSUNG HERO is the personal biography of Paul Robinson who is the current team and club captain of Birmingham City Football Club – The Blues! My Team! For the Watford, West Bromwich Albion, Bolton Wanderers and Leeds United fans reading this book please rest assured that on the advice of Steve Caron, Managing Director of DB Publishing Limited I have tried to be even-handed in writing Paul's biography in terms of giving equal coverage across the teams he has played for during his career. I hope I have achieved this requirement.

Robbo at Birmingham City's training ground on the day of signing for The Blues

Paul or 'Robbo' as he is known within the football community, has enjoyed a great career as a professional footballer and will have amassed over 700 senior appearances by the time you are reading this book.

Football, at the highest level, is fast losing its connection with the workingman and woman; no longer is football dependent on match day receipts, Bovril and meat pie sales or programme revenues. Attendance levels are subject to enormous competition from satellite television channels, which enable the football fan to watch professional football from home and abroad virtually twenty-four hours, seven days a week.

No longer are the majority of players home grown with an understanding of what is important to their clubs – most in the Premier League and Championship were born and raised in Europe, South America, Africa and the Far East and have little in common with the fans in terms of culture, attitude and lifestyle.

Long gone is the time when players were seen as blokes just like the fans, who just happened to have a skill which meant they got a better wage at the end of the week. The gap between the player and the fan has developed into a deep ravine.

So in this scenario, which will only grow in size during the next decade as player's wages continue to rise, and sponsorship deals and media rights get to become even more valuable, it is refreshing to realise that there are a few players left, 'throwbacks', if you like, to a recent past when the game and the supporters still meant something to the players. Paul Robinson epitomises all that is great about the remaining vestiges of English football:

- A total commitment to giving 100% for the duration of every match.

- A lifestyle choice, which has meant that his physical and mental capabilities have sustained a first team career of nearly 20 years.

- A desire to maximise his footballing abilities – for the good of himself and his family, whilst giving his employers excellent value for their money.

- A determination and single mindedness to do as well as possible for as long as possible in a game he clearly enjoys and loves.

'ROBBO' epitomises what true football fans want from every player that pulls on their team's shirt: total commitment to the cause, 100% effort and a 'never-say-die' attitude. This 'never-say-die' attitude has lead Paul to receive some yellow cards, a few red cards and become involved in two incidents involving fellow professional footballers: Stewart Talbot and Damien Johnson which have resulted in a bad reputation amongst opposition fans. However unlike the likes of Roy Keane (the Alf-Inge Haaland incident comes to mind), Robbo has never gone onto the field of play with the intention of hurting an opponent – his sole intention is always to win the ball for his team.

There are a number of footballers, Graham Souness, Lee Bowyer, Lee Carsley, Craig Bellamy, Joey Barton and Robbie Savage, to name just a few footballers who suffer abuse from opposition supporters based on their reputation (deserved or otherwise), but given the chance those very same fans would love to have them in their team – Robbo is one of that number – a true 'Unsung Hero'

Paul Peter Robinson was born on 14 December 1978 in Watford, which means this Sagittarian will be 36 years old when the 2014–15 season ends.

By which time 'Robbo' will have accumulated nearly 700 senior appearances in his career – not bad for a professional footballer who acknowledges that. 'I'm not skilful, I admit that, I haven't got the ability of other players, but some players haven't got my heart and the way I encourage players around me not to throw the towel in when the going gets tough. That's the way I was brought up and what I was born to do and what I will do until I hang my boots up'. (Reference: *Made In Brum* Fanzine – 30 January 2014)

With a physique befitting a tough-tackling defender of 5 feet 9 inches and 11 stone 7 pounds (1.75 metres and 75 kg for our younger readers)

(Note: www.bcfc.com in Paul's Player Profile, it suggests he is 12 stone 7 pounds!) his professional career has seen him wear the shirts of Watford, West Bromwich Albion, Bolton Wanderers, Leeds United and Birmingham City.

For the reasons detailed within his biography, 'Robbo' never achieved Full International status but he is immensely proud to have worn the England shirt on three occasions for the Under 21 team in 1999.

This is my seventh book on football and its players:

1. *THE BLUES – GREAT GAMES – GREAT TEAMS – GREAT PLAYERS* – self-published in 2006.

2. *GIL MERRICK* – published by Breedon Books in 2009.

3. *50 GREATEST MATCHES – BIRMINGHAM CITY* – published by Breedon Books in 2009.

4. *JACKIE SEWELL* – published by DB Publishing in 2010.

5. *MODERN DAY HEROES – BIRMINGHAM CITY* – published by DB Publishing in 2011.

6. *BAD BLOOD – BIRMINGHAM CITY v ASTON VILLA* – published by DB Publishing, an imprint of JMD Media, in 2013.

As with my previous books I have tried with *Robbo – Unsung Hero* to give the reader new interesting material rather than regurgitate the same facts under a different format.

Preface

My original idea was to write a book to record the fact that in 2015, Birmingham City Football Club celebrates the 140th anniversary of its formation back in 1875. The book had the working title of *Unsung Heroes* and was to be a history of all the successful captains of The Blues since 1930.

As always before 'putting pen to paper' I needed to draft what the structure of the book would be, and what the content might be for each section.

As with my previous books I needed someone to write a Foreword, someone with a connection to the content and who would be known to the readers. Previous writers of Forewords for my books were Malcolm Page (*Gil Merrick*), Peter McParland (*Jackie Sewell*), Ian Clarkson (*50 Greatest Matches*), Mike Wiseman – Honorary Vice President of Birmingham City Football Club (*Modern Day Heroes*) and Malcolm Stent – Entertainer (*Bad Blood*).

On this occasion my choice was obvious, could I persuade Paul Robinson to write the Foreword for *Unsung Heroes*? Thanks to the efforts of Andy Walker (Media & Communications Manager – Birmingham City Football Club) an interview with Paul was organised for Tuesday 22 July 2014 at the Wast Hills Training Ground to talk about the concept of the book.

I discussed with Paul the proposed format of the book and he was sufficiently interested in the idea to agree to contribute to the Foreword section. After more discussions I was delighted to agree to expand the chapter devoted to him in *Unsung Heroes* so that it became a mini biography.

Once I had researched Paul's career to date I realised that a chapter in *Unsung Heroes* would be inadequate to reflect what he had achieved in English football. At a meeting in Costa Coffee, Henley-in-Arden, which has been our regular meeting spot throughout the process, Paul and I decided that subject to approval from the publisher we would engage together to write a full-blown biography entitled *ROBBO – UNSUNG HERO* with Paul becoming my joint author. The Publisher agreed and here you are with a copy of the book of which both Paul and I are immensely proud. This decision did mean that my original book idea needed a new title – it became *THE LEADERS – BIRMINGHAM CITY FOOTBALL CLUB* and was published at the same time as *ROBBO – UNSUNG HERO.*

WHY 'UNSUNG HERO?'

Football clubs like Watford, West Bromwich Albion, Bolton Wanderers, Birmingham City and all those other clubs outside of the Premier League do not dominate the sports sections of the media. Add to this the favouritism of the press towards the London, Manchester and Liverpool teams and it is easy to understand how the 'star' players of these featured clubs become 'heroes' overnight in the eyes of football fans across the nation and overseas. Not so for players like Robbo, there is no one singing their praises – so they gain their Hero status by:

- Delivering consistently good performances – rarely less than seven out of ten game after game.

- Acknowledging the importance of the fans and their clubs in every way – never refusing a photograph or an autograph or asking for a transfer once a contract is in place.

- Taking a pride in wearing the shirt!

Included in *ROBBO – UNSUNG HERO* are 16 games that Paul has selected to feature in his biography because they were either significant for the clubs concerned or Paul himself:

MEMORABLE GAMES INDEX

No.	Team	Opposition	Date	Page
1	Watford	Port Vale	27 April 1994	49
2	Watford	Birmingham City	16 May 1999	52
3	Watford	Birmingham City	20 May 1999	55
4	Watford	Bolton Wanderers	31 May 1999	58
5	Watford	Liverpool	14 August 1999	66
6	Watford	Southampton	13 April 2003	69
7	West Brom Albion	Aston Villa	10 April 2005	94
8	West Brom Albion	Portsmouth	15 May 2005	97
9	West Brom Albion	Birmingham City	29 October 2006	102
10	West Brom Albion	Derby County	28 May 2007	107
11	West Brom Albion	Portsmouth	6 April 2008	110
12	Bolton Wanderers	Stoke City	17 April 2011	127
13	Birmingham City	Bristol Rovers	14 January 2014	158
14	Birmingham City	Sheff Wednesday	15 March 2014	161
15	Birmingham City	Bolton Wanderers	3 May 2014	166
16	Birmingham City	Bournemouth	25 October 2014	170

Foreword

By Kevin Phillips

I have known ROBBO since our days at Watford. I was there from 1994-95 season through to 98-99 and then our paths crossed again at The Hawthorns when I was there from 06-07 and 08-09. We've shared some great times on and off the pitch with plenty of laughs along the way! Oh and by the way I do not have a middle name, so where this 'Mark' came from I will never know, as none of my relatives are called Mark but it is used everywhere: Wikipedia, Sky Sports Football Year books, Birmingham City – The Complete Record and Birmingham City – Modern Day Heroes by a certain author known as Kev Dixon! (Oops sorry Keith.)

As a professional non-league footballer I joined Watford at the age of 21 to find that the sIxteen-year-old Paul Robinson was emerging from his apprenticeship at Vicarage Road. The five-year age gap and the difference in our individual footballing status at the club meant that initially we were nothing more than teammates. In those days, unlike today there was a definite 'them and us' culture between full-time professionals and the youngsters. Occasionally we would bump into one another and exchange a few words but nothing more than that.

Our friendship blossomed eight years ago when we were both playing for West Bromwich Albion, up until that time our paths had crossed as opponents and we would simply acknowledge each other as ex-Hornets. When I joined the Baggies I was pleased to see him in the squad and whilst initially we were just work colleagues eventually our contacts increased and we began to spend some social time together with our wives and families.

The two years we both spent at The Hawthorns were for me the best part of my career and I am sure Robbo will feel the same. The squad was close knit, we shared a great understanding and togetherness and that sort of rubbed off on Robbo and me. Our friendship showed itself at a barbecue I was hosting one Sunday at my home, we were very relaxed and had had a few drinks when we decided to dye our hair blonde. One thing about Robbo is that he can be a bit 'crackers' and on this occasion he was 'up for the crack'.

We did it there and then. Julie, my wife got some bleach and doused us in the stuff and then put cling film on our heads whilst the bleach worked. No problem at his stage but the cling film got tighter on our heads over time and our heads started to burn. Julie told us not to worry as the burning and the tightness would stop, which eventually it did but our hair was white!!!

When we went into training the following week Tony Mowbray, the gaffer at the time, and the lads 'hammered' us for being so stupid but it paid off – why? It coincided with us going on a winning streak so we carried on dyeing our hair until the run came to an end. Albion supporters will remember that my goal celebration involved Robbo coming over to me and we would rub each other's heads.

The blonde hair goal celebration

As a player Robbo was, and still is the worst loser in the game, he just has to win. He is known for his toughness and never shirking a tackle but he was a good footballing left-back and sometimes his skill is overlooked when people talk about him.

He is tough and not afraid to get involved when he needs to stand up for himself or a teammate. Whenever I played against him I would warn my teammates not to go near him unless you really had to because he is a top professional.

His confidence in his own ability comes from the fact that he has looked after himself physically and trains the way he plays, which can sometimes bring moans from his colleagues when on the training pitch.

He is a leader of men – never afraid to tell the truth when he has to and if a teammate is not doing it on or off the pitch he will let them know in no uncertain terms. Paul will make a great manager and/or coach because he listens and then offers good advice, which are also great qualities to have in a friend.

He is a good friend to me because he cares about the people close to him and is extremely patient. On occasions I have called him up and he just listens and lets me get things off my chest, which is a real help.

Currently as senior professional at Birmingham City he gets involved with the younger players who want the benefit of his patience, listening skills and good advice. Because of the type of person he is, he knows what to keep in confidence and what to filter out to the management team.

As friends and players we have shared two major disappointments in our careers and both when we were wearing the blue and white stripes of Albion. In my first season (2006–07) we lost to Derby County in the First Division Play-off Final, even though we were the better team on the day and throughout the season, couple that with the defeat in the FA Cup semi-final to Portsmouth at Wembley on 6 April 2008. As friends we were devastated as was the whole squad.

Because we are footballing friends it is sometimes difficult to determine whether his action is due to his passion for football or his friendship. For example when I was leaving West Bromwich Albion, the night before the day I had agreed to sign for Birmingham City, Robbo called me to say that at the eleventh hour he had managed to persuade Jeremy Peace and Gary Megson to meet my demands linked to a new contract, having refused to agree to my terms previously. Whilst I appreciated Paul's intervention on my behalf it was too late, as I had given my word to Alex McLeish and the management team at St Andrew's. Naturally he was disappointed but on the night after making my debut for Birmingham City he called me to congratulate me on scoring on my first appearance for the Blues, indicating that I should still be scoring for The Baggies! (For the record: 9 August 2008 v Sheffield United at St Andrew's 1–0 in front of a crowd of 24,019.)

We share a number of interests: Lager – Indian Food (I remember us being in a restaurant in Birmingham at 3.30 in the morning when I fell asleep over my meal or was it … in it!) – Golf (we play most of the decent local courses; The Belfry and The Forest of Arden etc.) and our love for our families.

Paul and I both have four children whilst he has four boys I have Alfie (aged nine who is a Number 10/9 with Derby County), Toby (aged 13 who is a midfielder with Wolverhampton Wanderers), Toby's twin sister Tia (who loves horse riding) and last but not least Millie who at 17 is an apprentice hairdresser.

Career Profile:

Kevin Phillips was born on 25 July 1973 in Hitchin, Hertfordshire, although he began his footballing career as a trainee with Southampton, staying there for six years, four as a schoolboy, before becoming an apprentice in 1989. As a youth, Phillips played at right-back as he was believed to be too small to play in a forward position. As a full-back he made two appearances for The Saints' reserve team in 1990 before being released by manager Chris Nicholl. Disappointed but not disheartened he joined the semi-professional ranks of Baldock Town in the close season preceding the 1991–92 season. Although still a defender an injury crisis meant that Ian Allinson, the manager at the time had to play him as a striker, which resulted in him scoring twice in his first game. How grateful is Kevin and English football for that decision!

He moved to Watford in December 1994, establishing himself in the first-team squad at the end of the 1994–95 season. A serious foot injury kept him out of the Hornets team that was relegated from the First Division the following season. In July 1997 he joined Sunderland for a fee of £325,000 as part of the re-building programme following the Black Cats relegation from the Premiership. He became the first Sunderland player since Brian Clough in the 1961–62 season to score 30 goals in a season, registering 35 goals in all competitions. Despite another serious injury his performances at Roker Park gained him an international call-up for England, managed by Kevin Keegan, in a friendly against Hungary. In 1999–2000 his goal-scoring exploits earned him both the Premier League Golden Boot and European Golden Boot awards. He broke Sunderland's post-war goal-scoring record in January 2001 when he scored his 104th goal for the club. In August 2003 with Sunderland relegated to The Championship he re-joined Southampton for a fee of £3.25m. He stayed for two years before moving to Villa Park signing a two-year deal with Aston Villa for a fee of £1m. On August 22 2006 he signed for West Bromwich Albion for a fee of £700,000 and scored his 200th League goal in a 1–1 draw with Crystal Palace on 13 March 2008, going on to help The Baggies secure promotion to the Premier League as Champions of The Championship. He was chosen along with Robbo and Jonathan Greening to be included in the Professional Footballer's Association Championship Team of the Year. At the end of the season he signed a two-year deal with Birmingham City scoring in the final match of the 2008–09 season against Reading, thereby helping to secure promotion for The Blues to the Premier League. He was an unused substitute in the Carling Cup victory over Arsenal at Wembley in 2011, thereby gaining his first winners' medal in a cup competition. He moved to Blackpool as Birmingham City were relegated to The Championship where he had two seasons before following manager Ian Holloway to Crystal Palace initially on loan before signing a one-year contract at the start of the 2013–14 season. Veteran Kevin Phillips scored the only goal as Crystal Palace deservedly defeated Watford in a tense Championship Play-Off Final at Wembley. The 41-year-old, a loser in three previous play-off finals, struck from the penalty spot at the end of the first half of extra time it was a superb penalty kick into the top corner On 15 January 2014 he signed a short-term playing contract with Leicester City staying on as striker mentor when he finally retired as a player. He made eight international appearances but surprisingly failed to score.

Acknowledgements

My thanks go to a number of people: Andy Walker and Colin Tattum who have both served as 'Head of Media and Communications – BCFC' (Note: Andy moved in to a similar communications role within The Football Association in December 2014) during the writing of the book.

Steve Caron and his team at DB Publishing and JMD Media for getting the book edited, proofread, printed and published.

My Bluenose friends – Mike O'Brien for the use of his archives and Mick Sherry for his meticulous proof-reading skills.

Special thanks go to Paul's family: Caroline, Luke, Jamie, Archie and Dexter for letting me into their home so that I could access their private photo albums, Paul's memorabilia and the scrapbook which Caroline started when they first 'got together'. This access enabled me to get a real insight into Paul as a person as well as a professional footballer. I also witnessed first-hand the importance to him of his family.

Thanks also to Mel and Sandra, Paul's Mum and Dad who loaned me their scrapbook collection.

Thanks to my family for supporting me: Julie, Holly and Harry (my photographer on match day – see Chapter Ten); Matt, Caleb and Amy; and Ben.

1.

'What's it all about?'

Paul recalls: I had been approached previously about writing my life story but it had never really appealed, I guess I thought I was not that type of personality. When I met Keith for the first time it was to discuss my contributing the Foreword to his book THE LEADERS – BIRMINGHAM CITY – a task that I have achieved successfully. During our discussions he suggested that writing my biography would be something worth doing, if only for my four sons to be able to say to their children 'this is what your Grandad did!' So here we are!

As I think all the subjects of a biography or autobiography say, the process has been 'interesting' – re-living your life's experiences from a different age gives you a unique opportunity to analyse your actions. Whilst you cannot change the circumstances it does allow you to put things into context and justify what happened. I have had the opportunity to review my career from a different perspective and for that I am grateful.

In this book I will be giving my opinion and answering a few questions on subjects as diverse as:

- Can I pick a team made up of the best players with whom I played? (See Chapter Seven.)

- Can I pick a team made up of the best players I played against? (See Chapter Seven.)

- Who are the Top Ten players in my position? (See Chapter Seven.)

- Who do I admire outside of football?
  (See Chapters Seven and Eight.)

- Foreign Players – How have they influenced and changed the
  English game? (See Chapter Eight.)

- What happens on a match day? (See Chapter Ten.)

- How is training conducted? (See Chapter Ten.)

- Video technology? (See Chapter Eight)

- What career would I have had if I had not been a footballer?
  (See Chapter Seven)

As always, when I have been asked a question my responses have been
honest. I hope you enjoy my answers.

To have played against some of the world's best players like Cristiano
Ronaldo, Wayne Rooney and David Beckham, is not something that every
footballer can say. But I have been incredibly fortunate to have had the
opportunity to play against some of the most talented players ever to grace
a football pitch whilst wearing the shirts of Watford, West Bromwich
Albion and Bolton Wanderers in England's Premier League.

And here I am in my thirty-seventh year and still people who are
important to me are being respectful of the job I do:

In the Official Match Day programme for the Birmingham City
Home fixture with Reading on 13 December 2014, Michael Mor-
rison was the featured player for interview by Peter Lewis the
Blues News editor. Peter asked the question, 'Do you feel as though
you're building up a good understanding and partnership with
Paul Robinson in the centre of defence?' Michael replied: 'Yes. I

think it works well with him being a left-sider and me coming in and playing the right. He's very experienced and vocal. You know exactly where he's going to be because we're both talking and that's a big part of any position in football, especially at centre-half. If you can get that good relationship then it makes a massive difference.' (Note: Match Result – Birmingham 6 Reading 1.)

In the *Birmingham Mail* Friday 12 December 2014 under the headline 'ROBBO GIVEN TIME TO GET OVER INJURY' The Blues Manager Gary Rowett was reported as saying, 'I am giving Birmingham City captain Paul Robinson every chance to prove his fitness before tomorrow's game with Reading.' The Blues manager revealed today the veteran defender needed several stitches in his foot during half-time of the defeat at Blackpool the previous Saturday. The injury was sustained in a tackle with Seasiders' striker Steve Davies; a challenge Rowett felt was worthy of a caution that resulted in Robinson being restricted in training this week. However it went unpunished – despite the fact that David Coote showed seven yellow cards. Rowett said, 'Davies just caught him early on in the game. I actually spoke to the referee about it afterwards and felt that it was probably a worse tackle which didn't get booked other than lots of other tackles which got booked and were nowhere near as bad as that. Paul ended up with five or six stitches in his foot at half time. I think even Robbo said he should have come off if the truth be known, if he was being really honest. But the type of pro and character he is, that's not an option for him. He soldiered through. This week it has been tight and sore as is often the case, it's right on the bone of his left foot. I don't see it as too much of an issue but we've not wanted him to train and open it up early in the week so we are trying to leave it as late as we can.' (Robbo passed a fitness test and lead his team to a 6–1 home win.)

Born and bred in Watford, I came through the ranks at Watford FC, making over 200 appearances for my local team during a seven-season stint at the club. I was part of the team that achieved promotion to the Premier League and I am led to believe in all humility that I am regarded as one of the best left-backs that the Hornets have ever had to date.

I then moved to West Bromwich Albion in October 2003, and never made less than 32 appearances in a season for the Baggies, during a six-season spell at the club. I helped the team achieve promotion to the Premier League and was part of the Baggies squad that made the 'great escape' from relegation in 2005.

Moving to Bolton Wanderers before the start of the 2009–10 season – initially on loan – I linked up with former West Bromwich Albion manager Gary Megson. My move was made permanent at the end of the season and I went on to enjoy two more successful seasons with the Trotters in the Premier League.

After a loan spell at Leeds, I joined my present club, Birmingham City in September 2012 on a one-month contract. My performances for the Blues were good enough for me to be rewarded with a contract extension till the end of the season.

At the end of the 2012–13 season, I got a further one-year contract and was handed the captain's armband for the 2013–14 Championship season.

Obviously I learnt the game from a young age. I watched it on the TV. Watching FA Cup Finals, World Cup Finals and I just wanted to play football on the biggest stage I could as often as I could and that drove me to, sort of, decide that I wanted to be a footballer and I wanted to achieve great things in life.

Initially I started off up front when I was younger and then I progressively made my way back as I got older. I went from up front to left-wing and then to left-back.

My current personal highlight, is obviously, my Great Escape with Birmingham City. Obviously at the moment (July 2014) that stands out for me, I mean I did it with West Bromwich Albion whilst I was there but the Birmingham one was just an unbelievable feeling knowing that it was going down to the last game and what it all meant to everyone.

I love being the captain here at Birmingham City and it is a new experience towards the end of my career, as I have never been an appointed captain at any of my previous clubs. It gives me great responsibility. I mean, if the players want to talk to me about certain things, they can, because they know I'm always there to listen. I really love working with the young lads and trying to help them improve and it works because they are so keen to learn – just me listening to them helps them. It gives me that responsibility that I want, because obviously, when I decide to hang up my boots, I want to go into coaching or management. As I want to go that route, my role as captain has set me on a great learning curve. I have always tried to set a good example both on and off the pitch – both as a professional footballer and a person. My family, who are the most important thing to me, expect me to set a good example for my family and in my work. So to set a good example to my kids off the pitch is the most important thing.

The Premier League is fantastic. It's the best league in the world, so you want to play in it. You get all the world-class players playing in it and to play against those players is incredible. Imagine when my sons have grown up and they will be able to watch me playing against the likes of Ronaldo, Rooney and all the other top quality players that I have played against, it will be a surreal moment for them. You have to pinch yourself sometimes that you've actually played against that player, in that week. So, it's something that you can dream of. I mean, you always dream of playing at the highest level and playing against the best clubs in the world and I've been lucky enough to do that.

Fans often ask me who is the best player I have played against and the answer is so tough because there have been so many. But I would say (Cristiano) Ronaldo, although Beckham, when I first played against him, was probably one of the hardest players to mark because you couldn't mark him. You never knew where he was positionally. But Ronaldo was on another planet, he was so strong, quick and physically he could blow you away in a space of a couple of seconds with just his movement and skill. Ronaldo without a shadow of a doubt is the best player that I have played against.

Being a professional footballer is a job that I love doing, but it takes a lot of dedication, a lot of drive and a lot of passion. I have dedicated my life to it. So for me, the advantage of it is just loving the job that I do. It's going out every time with a smile on my face and enjoying my football as much as possible. There are some disadvantages; you're always going to get the negative press that is around and certain things that go out about you. But that's just part and parcel of life and part and parcel of the game. You're always going to get negatives with the positives. Sometimes it can go over the top a little bit with fans, their reactions and the way that they can personally come for you. But as they say, it is how you deal with it that shows your own personal qualities, what I try to do is block out as much as I can, however, with social media these days, it is very easy for your family and friends to read things about you which are negative opinions. For your children to read or hear things that people have said about their dad is not a nice thing for them to experience. Here's an example when I was at The Albion; four of us used to play head tennis after training; Geoff Horsfield, Neil Clement, Russell Hoult and myself. It was just a bit of fun, but it got reported that we were playing for £60 per point – which was not only inaccurate, but what impression did it give to the Baggies' supporters!

My approach to the game is relatively simple, I work on what I believe I am good at and continue to strive to be better in each training session and game, there is always room for improving your game. Obviously my main aim is to go out and enjoy myself as well, because that's what I also believe is important. Enjoy it and make the most of it as much as I can. I watch and study opposition players, the ones that I am going to come up against and studying their movements and qualities, what positions you can get yourself into and work on that in my head and work on that on the training pitch. That's one of the most important things, preparation on the training pitch, working hard to be the best defender I can be, knowing what player I am coming up against at the weekend and that I am going to get the better of him.

I think I have made the most of the opportunities I have been given. It's such a driven sport. You know you've got to have that drive, you've got to have that passion and you've got to have that desire to become the best player you can be. Technically I may not the most skilful, but what I do have is the heart and drive to want to be the best at what I do and I want to prove people wrong that said to me that I wasn't good enough.

2.

'The Future?'

My contract with Birmingham City Football Club expires in June 2015 when this book will have been published and deemed a success or not and I will be in my 37th year. So what does the future hold?

I will definitely carry on playing for as long as I can; throughout my career I have had to find ways to compensate for my lack of height and pace. Therefore I have had to develop different techniques to allow me to play professional football at the highest level.

As Ray Wilkins said on Talk Sport in an interview with Alan Brazil on 20 October 2014, 'I lacked pace throughout my career but I was never exposed because I did the first two yards in my head.'

I know exactly what 'Wilko' means by that; if I am playing against a six foot plus forward I know I cannot beat him in a 'jumping for the ball' competition, but I can use my experience to get to the ball first so that his height advantage is reduced – if I am playing against a fleet-footed wing-back then I can judge the trajectory and pace of the ball such that I can physically compete in the space where he becomes dangerous to my team.

I am not sure that I could drop down the divisions to continue play-ing, but who knows what the future holds but the first person to know when I am 'past it' will be me!

Coaching is something that definitely appeals to me, I already have my U.E.F.A. 'B' Licence and I will be working on getting an 'A' licence in the summer of 2015 either in Ireland or at St George's Park in Staffordshire where they run two-week long sessions. It could take a year to complete at a cost of between £4,000 and £6,000.

I really enjoy helping the young players who are constantly asking for advice on what they should do in certain circumstances, what I think of this and that – it is part of my footballing life and I will never tire of trying to help young players achieve their ambitions.

Perhaps I will follow the example of my very good friend Kevin Phillips who has had the opportunity of joining the coaching staff and demonstrating what he can do at Leicester City, if I can achieve this at Birmingham City then that would be fantastic!

I very much work on the basis that you should learn all the time you are in the game and based on this philosophy when I move into coaching/management, I will try and emulate the experiences I had at Watford under Graham Taylor and Ray Lewington, not forgetting Kenny Jackett who guided me through the Youth system, which has instilled my views on how important grass roots football is for young players.

As well as from a professional point of view I have high aspirations on the personal front for my family. Being a professional footballer gives you a lot more time than the average workingman to spend with your wife and children. I met my wife Caroline when she was 20 and I was 18 years of age. We were introduced by a close friend of Caroline's – Kate Holmes. On our first date I had forgotten to make a dinner reservation at any of the local restaurants and having failed to find somewhere that could fit us in we settled for kebab and chips in the car! It sounds corny, but it truly was love at first sight and four years later she became my wife. We have been blessed with four beautiful sons; she is the perfect mother and my soul mate. Together we have experienced the highs and lows of football, I'm very fortunate to have met her so early on in my career.

My four boys are all into their sport; the eldest Luke at 12 plays rugby and football, whilst 8-year-old Jamie is working with the Blues' Under 9s and Archie, 5 and Dexter, 3 attend football training camps.

I believe one of the major reasons why I have been as successful as I have, exceeding most of the expectations I had as a young man, is down to having a constant deep inner belief in myself. I inherited a down to earth attitude from my Mum, Sandra and Dad, Mel who are both very loyal and loving people. Thanks to both of you. Dad works as a Head Barman in a local public house in Watford, whilst my mum Sandra works part-time in the nearby paper shop. I have two older siblings; Mark who is a carpenter and Joanne who works as a receptionist.

All my family were very supportive when I was growing up and my Dad did, what I do for my boys by accompanying me to all my training sessions and games, as well as offering positive advice. I should also add that my in-laws, Colin and Denise have always been extremely supportive to Caroline, our boys and me.

My first school was Holyrood Juniors followed by St Michael's Catholic High School in Garston, my best subjects were games and P.E. so it was inevitable that sport would be my career. My P.E. teacher, John Ridgewell was great for me, realising that I had great sporting abilities he encouraged me to focus my talents – a great mentor. I was lucky to be as supported as I was by John and the Headmaster – Mr Morgan (at that age I think everyone thought that Headmasters and Headmistresses did not have Christian names!) who was a Glasgow Celtic fan and had great presence around the school, but I remember him as a fair and reasonable man. They realised that I was determined to be a professional sportsman and therefore did not overly chastise me for my lack of interest in other academic subjects, which could have been the case at other schools.

As well as football I excelled at Athletics competing in the 110 metres Hurdles, 400 metres Hurdles. High Jump (that's where I got my 'spring' from and it still helps me hold my own as part of a defensive back four!) and Javelin.

Regarding other academic subjects I did not do to badly gaining 'B' grades in English Language, Geography and History alongside an 'A' grade in … you've guessed it Physical Education.

I went back to St. Michael's on 17 July 2001 as Guest of Honour for its Physical Education Awards and Presentation Ceremony (Inspiring the athlete in all). A student called James Major won the 'Paul Robinson Award for Football'. A copy of the programme cover appears on page 32.

My attitude to school could be summed up as 'a lack of interest' and that was probably reinforced with my other teachers as I was often in 'trouble' because of my joking around! I must have driven the school bus drivers mad as I used to 'play up' both to and from school with my mates, notably Ben Cowen and Chris Aldridge. At that time I was part of a really tightknit group of boys and girls who all got on with each other really well.

As well as playing for school teams I was a forward for S & K United under nines prior to me starting to train with Watford when I was nine years of age. Initially, I had no interest in watching football and it was not until a local junior football scout called Bob Harman, who was a fanatical Tottenham Hotspur fan, took me to White Hart Lane that I watched a professional football match and Glenn Hoddle instantly became my footballing hero. As well as Hoddle my other boyhood heroes were Paul Gascoigne, Stuart Pearce and Maldini.

After that I used to watch Watford as a boy and I remember players like Wilf Rostron, Kenny Jackett and John Barnes, but Luther Blissett was my idol because he was scoring all the goals.

The highlight of my school footballing days was when I captained St Michael's football team to the English Schools' Football Association Under-16s Cup Final at Prenton Park, the home of Tranmere Rovers in 1995.

I am not the only St Michael's old boy to become a professional footballer as Craig Mackail-Smith, the Brighton and Hove Albion striker followed me as pupil, albeit he is five years younger than me.

Golf has always been an interest of mine starting on Sunday mornings at Bushey Hall Golf Club where I was a member with my cousin John.

INSPIRING THE ATHLETE IN ALL.

Physical Education
Awards & Presentation
Ceremony 2001

St Michael's Catholic High School.

Guest of Honour:

Paul Robinson.
Watford Football Club.

Date: Tuesday 17th July 2001

Time: 6:30pm for 7:00pm start

'Bringing Christ to All and All to Christ'.

Back to School

3.

'Watford'

I have to thank the former Aston Villa boss, Graham Taylor for my big break in football. (Note: Graham Taylor had two spells as Watford manager: June 1977 to May 1987 when his record was Played 466 Won 210 Drew 114 Lost 142 Win Ratio 45.06% and Feb 1996 to June 2001 when his record was Played 275 Won 104 Drew 80 Lost 91 Win Ratio 37.82%).

He had some great qualities as a manager: man management, tactical awareness and was well organised and structured in everything he did at the football club, he set up roles for each position in the team so that the players knew exactly what they had to do and he had total trust in the team, there was never any interference during the game.

Graham was manager at the Hornets when we were crowned Division Two Champions in 1997–98 and Division One Play-Off Winners the following season and during our failed Premiership campaign, but that time under the former England boss had a big impact on my career. He was my first proper manager and gave me my big chance. I also played under Glenn Roeder (Note: July 1993 to February 1996 – Win Ratio 32.5%) and Kenny Jackett (Note: June 1996 to June 1997 – Win Ratio 34.8%), but it was Taylor who showed the faith in my ability to throw me into the first team and then give me a full season in the side. I came through at a time when Graham Taylor was giving a lot of the young lads a chance to come through the youth team and progress. I came through with nine other players, so it was a great era to be part of the club. It was a fantastic time for the town and for the club as we were always renowned as a small team, so to put Watford on the footballing map was fantastic.

It was great to work with Graham Taylor because he had such a wealth of experience from his time as England manager. He had a big influence on me when I was starting out and helped to make me the player I am today.

When I signed a professional contract in 1996, Watford was a member of the Football League Division Two, but because of where they were in the league it meant that I got my chance so much earlier than I would have had, had I been with a team in a higher league.

I made by debut at the age of 17 coming on as a second-minute substitute against local rivals Luton Town on 29 October 1996. I did not know at the time but that meant that I was the first Watford-born player to represent the club at senior level since Kenny Jackett. That game coming at such an early stage in my career made me the person and the player I am today, a bit fiery. I can remember it clearly; it was only two minutes in, Dominic Ludden pulled his hamstring pretty much straight away, but tried to play on. When he started limping people were telling me to go and warm up. I was nervous enough anyway but then two of my teammates from the youth team were on the bench with me and looked even more nervous than me! I knew there was a chance I would go on when I went to warm up, then I heard the manager calling me back over and he told me to get stripped quickly. My heart was thumping a bit! To be fair though it was excitement as much as nerves, I knew I was going on, so I just wanted to get on quickly and deal with anything that came my way. Of the game I remember bits and pieces. It was a strong, fiery game as derby games always are, although not quite as fiery as Wolves against The Albion or Blues versus Villa! Those are the games you really cherish and enjoy, but the fact it was my debut made it extra special. We drew that game 1–1 with Darren Bazeley getting a really late equalizer. I loved all the games against Luton Town, really every minute of them; they are even better when you win of course, so you can rub it in a bit! There is one game that sticks in my memory against The Hatters – the 4–0 game; that was a great game. I was sat on the bench that day and I was more scared sitting there than if I had been on the pitch! The fans were going mad, punching the dugouts and trying to get on the pitch but the police were doing nothing, they were getting bullied themselves, so we just sat there and expected the worst to happen. But it was a great day and a great result. I remember Peter Kennedy got a hat-trick in that game and he was winding their fans up with his celebrations, which meant they were getting even more aggressive! We were shouting at Pete to just head back to the halfway line and not towards the dugout! I absolutely loved those games, especially that one because of the way that we played and the result that we got made everyone so happy, especially the fans. I went on to make 12 more appearances that season so it was a really great start for me.

The first three seasons after I made my debut were great for the club after finishing mid-table in my first season we were Division Two Champions in season 1997–98 even though I was in and out of the side I was making a contribution as the manager played me when the side reverted to the 4-4-2 formation from our normal 3-5-2. Graham Taylor was in his second spell at the club coming in as Director of Football in February 1996 with Kenny Jackett as Head Coach, not long after that Graham took over as Manager with Kenny as his assistant. Then my football world changed because as a 19-year-old I was going to play in the top division of English football when we beat Bolton Wanderers in the Championship Play-Off Final. With the club playing 4-4-2, I became a regular half-way through the season and featured in the club's run to the play-offs. I made 32 appearances for Watford in their 1999–2000 FA Premier League season, and stayed with the club when they were relegated to Division One, making a further 124 league appearances for Watford in the second tier over the next four seasons.

At the end of the 1998–99 season I was voted by the Players and Staff into second position for The Young Player of The Season award. Gifton Noel-Williams (See Chapter Nine) won the award with Tommy Smith in third place. In the same season I was ninth in The Player of The Season award sponsored by the *Watford Observer*.

In 1998 Paul was the subject of a regular programme feature entitled 'Getting to know ...' Here are some of his responses as a 20-year-old:

If you had £50 to spare in your pocket, what would you do with it?
Buy my girlfriend Caroline something.

If you were stranded on a desert island, what three things would you want with you and why?
My girlfriend Caroline, a Television and beer.

If you could be anybody else for a day, who would it be and why?
Johnny Vaughan, because then I could get to wake up and see Denise Van Outen.

If you could change one thing about yourself, what would it be?
My ears, because they are a little bit big.

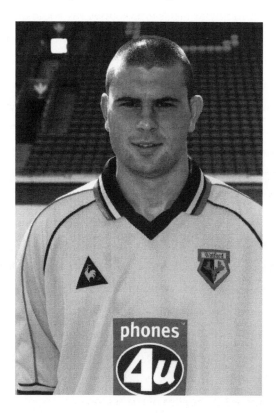

No Problem

Which one attribute of any of the other Watford players would you like more of?
Some of Wayne Andrews' pace.

If you could change any rule in football, what would it be?
I'd not change anything.

What is the oddest thing a fan has ever asked you to do?
A fan called me Tommy Mooney last year – God knows why, because I've got hair.

What is the funniest thing you have ever seen in a match you have played in?
The funniest thing that I have ever seen was when I was playing for my school team. One of our players got knocked out by the referee – hang on a minute, it was me! Well, it was funny afterwards.

Do you prefer Indian or Chinese – and what's your favourite dish!
Chinese – Crispy Aromatic Duck.

What is the biggest risk you have ever taken?
Taking my girlfriend out for a drink.

What is the best present you have been bought?
My Mum and Dad bought me a gold ring for my 18th birthday.

Who is the best looking woman on television or in films?
Denise Van Outen.

What is the best game of football you have played in?
Against Bradford at the start of the season.
(Note: After Watford secured a 1–0 victory over Bradford on 15 August

1998 Graham Taylor said 'The little boy Robinson, who I think is going to be a good player has got a chance and can say to himself "Hey, I've got a chance of being his (Graham Taylor's) first choice!"')

And what is the best game of football you've watched?
When Liverpool beat Newcastle 4–3

If you could go back and change one thing in your career, what would it be?
I wish I was born with a half decent right foot.

Who are the best and worst football commentators on TV or radio?
The best is Alan Hansen. The worst are Alan Brazil and Trevor Francis.

What would you sing at a karaoke night?
Wild Thing.

Do you do the shopping, cooking and cleaning?
No.

What frightens you?
Snakes give me the creeps.

Would you rather score the winner in a World Cup Final or win the National Lottery jackpot?
The World Cup Final winner.

What would you go to a fancy-dress party as?
A clown.

What job would you most like if you weren't a footballer?
Professional golfer.

What is the best piece of advice you could give to a young footballer?
Always listen to what's being said and enjoy yourself.

Paul's current World XI:
Seaman (England); Kafu (Brazil), Adams (England), Blanc (France),
Maldini (Italy); Laudrup (Denmark), Zidane (France), Gascoigne
(England), Denilson (Brazil); Batituta (Argentina), Owen (England).

Paul's personal top 11 compilation for Hornets' Hit List would be:
Wonderwall (Oasis) – Angels (Robbie Williams) – Jesus to a Child
(George Michael) – Don't look back in Anger (Oasis) – Purple Rain
(Prince) – Summer Nights (Cast of Grease) – Horny (Mousse T
featuring Hot'n Juicy) – Beachball (Nalin and Kane) – I can't help
myself (lucid) – Freak Me (Another Level) – Mysterious Times (Sash).

Graham retired at the end of the 1999–2000 season in May 2001 to be
replaced by Gianluca Vialli. (Note: From May 2001 to June 2002 Played 46
Won 16 Drew 11 Lost 19 Win Ratio 34.78%.)

The Italian connection with Gianluca resulted in Watford embark-
ing on a pre-season tour of Italy in August 2001. Paul was reported
at the time as follows: 'This summer to be playing against the likes of
Vieiri, Seedorf and Blanc, it is amazing. When the game starts you
are focussed and you don't tend to notice who you are up against.
But every now and then it does go through your mind who is in the
other team, and you can only learn from that sort of experience.
Laurent Blanc – I'll be watching him closely. He's world-class, he's
won the World Cup with France and I've played against him! The
only thing missing from the pre-season friendly with Inter Milan
was an appearance by Ronaldo. The game against Watford was
intended to be Ronaldo's long-awaited comeback game after his
right knee collapsed two years previously but he was not ready and

watched the game from the stand. I was gutted he did not play but I did get his autograph. That's the first autograph I have asked for since I became a professional, and I was proud to get it.' (Note: the game was lost 2–1 – the next game was in Genoa against Sampdoria, which resulted in another defeat, this time 4–0.)

The gaffer wanted to get us together and have a chance to get away from it a bit. The set up was like in the previous summer; it really sets you up for the season. In the Inter Milan game I was the only member of the back four who was not a new signing. It's been quite difficult for everyone to get to know everyone else, especially with a lot of different languages. There is also a new style of play to learn, but I think with every game we play, you can see that everything is coming together. My role has changed. I get a lot more of the ball from the 'keeper and the other defenders, and that has helped my confidence. The gaffer wants me to get forward when I can, and I like to do that. I like having the ball and I want to get inside the opposition half.'

He made several high-profile signings, and the wage bill at the club soared, with Vialli himself earning almost a million pounds a year. However, the season was disappointing, with the club finishing 14th in the division, and he was sacked after only one season, having refused to resign. He was replaced by Ray Lewington, now assistant to Roy Hodgson in the England International set up, who had come to the club the previous summer as Vialli's reserve team manager. (Note: From June 2002 to March 2005 Played 131 Won 42 Drew 36 Lost 53 Win Ratio 32.06%.) The type of football Vialli encouraged us to play was great. It's always good to learn different things off different managers and I really enjoyed my football. Unfortunately the money side of things didn't work out for the club. Some of the players that came in just didn't perform as was hoped, and players just didn't click with each other, which was really disappointing. Obviously the club suffered long term with the money problems. All in all it was a massive gamble and it backfired. Some of the players that were there at the time were maybe turning up just to pick up the money? For me you have to have a respect for your teammates, maybe there was a lack of that but it wasn't for me to say. That was down to the manager to do, and he has to see it and then put his foot down. I feel that he did put his foot down but those players stayed around and caused trouble for some of the others, I think that was the biggest problem; too many bad eggs causing trouble for all the others. The manager brought these people in expecting them to do a job but some of them just didn't do it. Ultimately that cost Gianluca his job, cost players money and more importantly it stopped the club from progressing because over the summer many of the Vialli's signings left the club. Ray had limited funds to strengthen the side. The extent of Watford's financial difficulties was exposed in the autumn, along with many League clubs, following the collapse of ITV Digital .The club was facing administration when the players and staff agreed a 12% wage deferral. Exacerbating the club's financial difficulties were the large payoffs they had had to make to Vialli and several players on terminating their contracts, and Vialli's decision to sue the club early in 2003. The club started the season well, however, despite the players having to agree to a pay-cut during October, and we finished in mid-table. Our unexpected run to the FA Cup semi-final generated vital cash. Vialli liked to play great football. The knowledge behind it and the tactical awareness is just amazing. The training is very technical; it's all about passing, possession, little five-a-sides, attacking, defending. Very in depth but without pressure, he wanted us to go out and enjoy our football. It just did not work out for anyone – the manager, the players, the club, the fans and me in particular as I was on the move!

Just scored the equaliser against rivals Luton Town

Graham Simpson Watford Chair stated on 9 October 2003:

'It is with great regret that the Board has accepted West Bromwich Albion's offer for Paul Robinson. No decision like this is taken lightly, but given our current position a six-figure sum represents significant income. This offer was totally unsolicited, Paul was not looking for a move and, as a club we weren't looking to move him on. Obviously this is not something Ray Lewington would want to do in an ideal world, but he understands the reasons behind the decision which was made by myself and the Board.'

Graham Simpson's reference to 'our current position' really started when Graham Taylor was replaced by Gianluca Vialli.

As Paul said at the time:

I was as surprised as anyone when Watford appointed Vialli as their new manager when The Gaffer made his announcement. I didn't think the club would go for someone as high profile, but I can't wait to start work with the former Italian star. The rumours started flying about towards the end of the season that they would get Vialli, but I didn't think they would get anyone of that standard. It was difficult for the last four or five weeks of the season when we knew Graham was leaving, but now everyone is looking forward to a new challenge. I think it's a fantastic appointment for the fans, players and everyone at the club. It's a new challenge and we've all got to knuckle down and work hard. We must fight for our places and try to challenge for promotion. Naturally I was slightly fearful of my future with nine players being placed on the transfer list, but last season I signed a four-year contract so that eased my worries. I'm always confident in my own ability and feel I've impressed in the games Vialli is supposed to have been watching, It's up to him if he doesn't like me when he comes in, but I know I will have to fight for my place. I feel I've got a year to impress and hopefully get in the Premiership, and then look forward to the remaining three years of my contract. I think Vialli will bring a different type of experience to the club. Graham obviously managed England, and it was great to work under someone who had managed the national side. But Vialli has played and managed at the top level – and he will bring different skills and attributes

to the job. I'm sure he will give it his best shot, and we'll be giving it our
best shot to help him out. Graham is going to be a hard man to replace, but
Vialli is not going to be scared – and although there will be pressure on his
shoulders in one respect, I don't think there will be in another way because
he has proved himself at the top level. He managed international players
at Chelsea but we have got internationals at our club – although they are a
different type of international. But I think the qualities he will bring to the
club will help improve the players we have.

Regrettably things did not work out as the article by David Bond entitled 'The cost of clearing up Vialli's mess' explains;

'Just two-and-a half years ago Watford, under the steady steward-
ship of Graham Taylor were among the high rollers of the cash-rich
Premiership. Today they are staring into a financial abyss following a gamble that went horribly wrong. Like a small-time punter
used to playing the slot machines down the local pub, Watford
were suddenly invited into the back room of a Las Vegas casino to
play with the big boys. They lost and were relegated. But despite all
the precedents of clubs that had gone before them and the loss of
Taylor as manager at the end of the 2001 season, Watford couldn't
resist one last card. That it turned out to be the joker, in the form
of Gianluca Vialli, is unfortunate. But now, as the collapse of ITV
Digital begins to bite, they are desperately slashing costs in an
effort to save the club. Things got so bad after the Italian's igno-
minious departure that the board closed the players' canteen and
asked the first-team squad to wash their own kit. Now the players
will probably club together and pay someone to do their laundry.

'Peter Fincham, a founder member of the Watford Independent
Supporters' Club and a contributor to internet club fanzine *Blind,
Stupid and Desperate* said, "After we were relegated and failed to
get back up, the club should have consolidated their losses. Instead

they brought in Vialli and gave him £5 million to spend on players. It was a one-year gamble that had to pay off, but didn't. It's a situation that makes me feel uncomfortable."

'It is a familiar tale, as other former Premiership clubs like Nottingham Forest and Sheffield Wednesday have found to their cost. But Watford can at least take comfort from the fact they aren't yet in Bradford City's shoes. The Yorkshire club was on the brink of disappearing from the Football League until yesterday when creditors reluctantly accepted a rescue package. But there are still grave fears for the future at Vicarage Road and yesterday's High Court ruling against the Football League in its legal battle against Carlton and Granada won't do anything to lift the spirits.

'What is perhaps so alarming is the speed with which Watford has gone from a club in £3m profit in 2000 to a club making pre-tax losses of £5.4m in 2001. Hazel O'Callaghan from the Watford Independent Supporters' Club said, "It took Graham Taylor four years to rebuild the club and, after he left, just one year to destroy it."

'Strangely, fans don't blame Vialli but the club's plc board for failing to keep closer control on the wages he was paying to players. However, the Italian's role is crucial to the crisis.

'Vialli's transfer expenditure certainly wasn't the cause of Watford's woes. He spent just over £1m net on new players in 2001–02 compared to Taylor's net spending of £3.85m the previous season.

'It was the salaries paid out to him, to the players brought in on free transfers and to backroom coaching staff that caused the problems.

'Ramon Vega was on just over £1m a year, or £19,000 a week, after joining from Tottenham Hotspur, Marcus Gayle, signed from Newcastle United for £900,000 was on £13,000 per week while Pierre Issa, Stephen Glass, Patrick Blondeau and Stephen Hughes were all on more than £10,000 a week.

'He brought in a host of coaches, fitness conditioners, nutritionists et al as he attempted to graft Premiership values on to the club. It was meant to guarantee a speedy return, but their annual wage bill was more than £8m, it was financial suicide.

'Turnover last year was just £10m and despite the huge sums being paid out, Watford finished 14th in the First Division last season after flirting with relegation. Vialli could not stop the malaise caused by the average performances of his so-called Premiership standard players. Instead of catapulting the club back to glory they adopted prima donna attitudes beyond their standing.

'One story has Vega contemptuously waving a £50 note on a regular basis as he strolled in late through the training ground gates. Most top clubs fine their players this much for the indiscretion.

'As a result, Vega, Issa and Blondeau have all now left the club as, of course, has Vialli, his team of coaches and assistant Ray Wilkins – all having been paid off for a cost of more than £4m. The much steadier hand of Ray Lewington is now manager with Nigel Gibbs, who has retired as a player after 20 years, taking up the role of reserve team manager.

'Times are tough. The reserve team are having to wear the first team's cast-off kit and there is no money to bring in new players. Sean Dyche the only signing of the summer on a free transfer from Millwall.

'With no more Premiership parachute payments to look forward to (they stopped in December 2001) and a dramatic reduction in TV income on the horizon, Watford's directors have agreed to take the hit. The question that concerns supporters now, however, is how will it be financed.

'Some believe a few of the Watford Leisure board's wealthiest directors. Such as acting Chairman Haig Oundjian and Nigel Wray, a former Nottingham Forest owner and until a few months ago owner of Saracens will buy more shares in the club in return for loans. Most fans want to believe the chief executive Tim Shaw; a lifelong supporter of the club, when he says the club has learned from its gamble and will bounce back. But he only owns 1.29 per cent of Watford Leisure. The biggest shareholder is Oundjian with 39.4 per cent of the shares but his motives have aroused suspicion since he first took control of the club in 1997.

'He owns his shares through an offshore trust called Penguin Overseas Associates. His link to the property developer Wray, who is blamed by Forest supporters for their financial plight, is a source of deep unease. The uncertainty surrounding the two men's motives increased in June 2001 when the club floated on the Alternative Investment Market. The move raised £4.9m valuing the club's parent company at about £20m. At that point the plan was to use the funds to help buy the freehold to Vicarage Road from the brewers Benskins and redevelop the old East Stand. A year earlier there had been talk of moving the club to a new site in Watford, but that was scrapped because of the high cost of land. The freehold was eventually bought for £4m, but all talk of redevelopment of the stand has been shelved as the club struggles to make ends meet. The club's market value is now just over £15m.

'Sir Elton John could see what was coming. He resigned as chairman in May, although the singer still owns 8.37 per cent of the shares in Watford Leisure. When anxious supporters asked Shaw why Watford were so keen to get their hands on the freehold of Vicarage Road, he told them it was to maximise revenues from catering and drinks sales, which previously went to Benskins. But with Wray involved, there are fears that if Watford's financial position worsens then there might be some on the board who will consider cashing in on the freehold and local land prices.'

MEMORABLE GAME 1

PORT VALE 1 – WATFORD 2 • 27 April 1994

Tommy Mooney's double strike boosted Watford's play-off hopes in a bad-tempered clash at Port Vale.

Mooney grabbed the winner on the hour after Tommy Widdrington's penalty for Vale had cancelled out Mooney's opener.

Watford's sixth successive victory enabled Graham Taylor's men to climb above Wolves and Bolton into fifth place and left Vale hovering precariously above the relegation zone. The match was badly marred by a competitive challenge by Paul Robinson on Stewart Talbot, which left the Vale midfielder with a compound fracture of his right leg. Referee George Cain incensed Vale by showing only the yellow card and Watford, who could easily have played most of the game with nine men, went on to claim three priceless points. Watford made a lively start and Michael Ngonge should have given them a sixth-minute lead when he shot wide from Mooney's cross. Vale responded with efforts from Martin Foyle and Alan Lee, but the game exploded into life after the visitors took a twenty-fourth minute lead. Robinson got the better of Talbot to pull the ball back for Mooney who swept home his fifth goal in as many games. The Watford fans had barely finished celebrating when Vale were awarded a penalty after Steve Palmer appeared to punch Lee. Referee Cain, after consulting a linesman, angered the home crowd by only booking Palmer before Tommy Widdrington dispatched the twenty-eighth minute spot kick. The Vale supporters were whipped into a frenzy just two minutes later when Robinson launched into his challenge on Talbot. There were angry exchanges between players with Vale skipper Neil Aspin needing lengthy treatment after being floored in a collision with Ngonge as a first half packed with ill feeling drew to a close. Aspin was soon in the thick of the action on the resumption as he made a brave last-ditch clearance to deny Nick Wright at close range. But Vale were caught cold on the hour when Mooney claimed his second goal after fastening onto a long clearance from Watford 'keeper Alec Chamberlain. Although Mooney's initial strike was blocked by Paul Musselwhite, the burly striker followed up to slide in the loose ball. Vale's Tony Rougier had the ball in the net only to be flagged offside before Brian Horton brought on Tony Naylor and Chris Allen in an attempt to pep up his attack. But it was Watford who went closest to scoring again when Peter Kennedy's long-range shot cracked against a post. Vale medical officer David Phillips confirmed Talbot had suffered a compound fracture of his right tibia and fibula.

Port Vale: Musselwhite, Aspin, Tankard, Brammer, Beesley, Eyre (Allen 71 minutes), Talbot (Snijders 33 minutes), Rougier, Lee, Foyle (Naylor 63 minutes), Widdrington.
Goal: Widdrington 28 minutes pen.

Watford: Chamberlain, Bazeley, Kennedy, Page, Palmer, Robinson, Ngonge, Hyde, Mooney, Johnson, Wright (Hazan 80 minutes).

Subs Not Used: Smith, Easton. Booked: Palmer, Robinson.
Goals: Mooney 24 and 60 minutes. • **Attendance:** 7,126
• **Ref:** G Cain (Bootle).

Stewart Talbot

The injury kept Talbot out of the game for 10 months needing a breakthrough motion fixation treatment to speed up the recovery process. Four years later he successfully sued Robinson and Watford F.C., both settling out of court for 'a substantial six-figure sum.' The six-figure payout was for potential loss of earnings as a result of the incident. Although Stewart Talbot – who went on to be the captain of Rotherham – resumed his career less than a year later, his lawyers argued that his subsequent earning ability had been damaged. A decisive factor in the settlement of Talbot's case, according to his solicitor, Russell Dutton, was the survey conducted by *The Independent* newspaper into footballers' wages, published in 2000. The survey was submitted as evidence in Talbot's case, which in the secretive world of football, Dutton regarded it as the best first-hand evidence of players' earnings. After its submission, the parties involved reached an out-of-court settlement. 'The survey was of great significance to the case,' said Dutton, the personal injury partner at Beswick's Solicitors. 'I believe it had a big effect on the settlement of this action and we are grateful to The Independent for its assistance.'

Talbot said: 'I never wanted to go to court but it seemed as if that's where it was heading until the survey was put forward. I'm just glad it's all over.'

As a result of his injuries, Talbot had six metal pins inserted in his leg, three below the knee and three above the ankle. He believed his career prospects had been damaged. When his contract with Port Vale expired in the summer of 2000, the best move he could find was to Rotherham, who had been promoted to the Second Division.

Talbot's legal action was against both Watford and Robinson. He argued that had the incident never happened, he would have been able to secure a better contract with a higher-paying club in 2000. The case was due to be heard in the Telford County Court. The no-liability settlement, for 'a substantial six-figure sum' according to Dutton, saved the case going to court.

The crux of the case, if and when it had been established whether a double fracture had harmed the players' prospects, was how much Talbot might have earned by moving to an average First Division club instead of Rotherham. The Independent's survey showed the average First Division wage in April 2000 was £128,000 per year, rising to £163,000 per year for players aged 27 to 28 years old. Talbot turned 27 in June 2000. He moved to a club just leaving the Third Division, where average wages were £37,000 in 2000, or £44,000 for a player of Talbot's age.

The wide-ranging survey, which was conducted with the assistance of the Professional Footballers' Association, received more than 600 responses from players.

MEMORABLE GAME 2

WATFORD 1 – BIRMINGHAM CITY 0 • 16 May 1999

*Nationwide League Division One Play-off
semi-final first leg at Vicarage Road*

Watford: Chamberlain, Bazeley, Palmer, Page, Robinson, Hyde, Johnson, Kennedy, Wright (Smart 67 minutes), Ngonge (Hazan 81 minutes), Mooney.
Unused Sub: Day.
Scorer: Ngonge.

Birmingham: Poole, Rowett, Grainger, Robinson (Ndlovu 69 minutes), Holdsworth, Johnson, McCarthy, O'Connor, Furlong, Bradbury (Adebola 45 minutes), Holland.

Unused Sub: Purse. • **Attendance:** 18,535.
• **Referee:** Clive Wilkes (Gloucester).

Bookings: 10 minutes – Page for a foul on Furlong; 19 minutes – Robinson throwing the ball away; 21 minutes – Furlong for diving; 33 minutes – Rowett for foul on Mooney; 59 minutes – Grainger for a foul on Wright; 70 minutes – Mooney for persistent fouling; 76 minutes Robinson for foul play –sent off as second bookable offence; 86 minutes –O'Connor for dissent.

Graham Taylor commenting on Robinson's sending off said: 'I have no complaints at all. You can't throw the ball away without risking a caution. Okay, a Birmingham player can hold onto the ball and walk away – that appears to be okay with the referee, but if you throw the ball away, you do run that risk. Paul was booked and was then on a knife-edge knowing that the next mistimed tackle would result in a sending off. He has to learn from these situations. He'll miss the game at St Andrew's. Obviously he is very, very low, but you have to learn. I put my arm around him and told him you threw the ball away son, what else can you expect. From then on you were on a knife-edge knowing the next mistimed tackle would earn you a red card. So he misses the game on Thursday, but he has to learn about his responsibility to the team. He is not just letting himself down; he is letting the team down. He must learn and I am sure he will because he is a bloody good player. So in one respect you put an arm around him and in the other, you are making him aware. The responsibility is to one another. He misses the game but we miss you, Robbo. It might cost us. Also if we go through it puts his Wembley appearance in jeopardy.'

Match Report:

In a game of changing fortunes Watford could have all but booked their place in the Division One Play-off Final but spurned a succession of chances. Then Graham Taylor's men, the outsiders of the play-off quartet (Note: At the end of the season Sunderland as Champions and Bradford City were automatically promoted leaving Ipswich Town (third), Birmingham City (fourth), Watford (fifth) and Bolton Wanderers (sixth) in the Play-offs.) were forced to hang on after Paul Robinson was sent off for a second offence after 76 minutes. Watford were given a flying start by Zaire international Michel Ngonge. He climbed above a suspect Birmingham defence to power in a five-yard header from Peter Kennedy's corner. Watford then had further chances. Northern Ireland international Kennedy was presented with a clear shot at goal from ten yards at the far post but missed the target. Then Kennedy, diving to meet a cross from Richard Johnson, sent his header beyond the far post. Birmingham who had to defend in numbers, pushed forward on the half hour. Paul Furlong, the former Watford striker, proved the biggest threat. He sent a snap shot from Gary Rowett's cross just wide of the target and then headed over when Steve Robinson centred. Watford finished the half squandering two further gilt-edged chances. When Alec Chamberlain cleared up field Ngonge challenged and the ball fell to Nick Wright who then lobbed over the 'keeper and the bar. A few minutes later Tommy Mooney chipped clear of the 'keeper but again cleared the bar. Mooney was unlucky early in the second half when he met Darren Bazeley's centre with a header which beat Kevin Poole but the ball struck the inside of the post and bounced out. Just before Robinson was dismissed he made a timely intervention after Chamberlain came out to the edge of his box and failed to claim a cross. Dele Adebola and Furlong went for the ball and it looked a certain equaliser but somehow Robinson managed to clear. His 77th minute tackle on Peter Ndlovu was reckless and the referee was left with no alternative but to show him a second yellow card. Birmingham, sensing the chance of a breakthrough, piled on the pressure but Watford stood firm with only one real scare. That was when a Rowett cross fell to the unchallenged Adebola and Furlong but they collided with each other and the opportunity was lost.

MEMORABLE GAME 3

BIRMINGHAM CITY 1 – WATFORD 0 • 20 May 1999

Nationwide First Division Play-off semi-final second leg at St Andrew's

Birmingham: Poole, Rowett, Grainger, Adebola (Holland 64 minutes), Holdsworth, Johnson, McCarthy (Purse 57 minutes), O'Connor (Bradbury 99 minutes), Furlong, Hughes, Ndlovu.
Sent Off: Holdsworth (54 minutes).
Booked: Holdsworth, Grainger.
Goal: Adebola 2 minutes.

Watford: Chamberlain, Bazeley, Kennedy, Page, Palmer, Gibbs, Ngonge (Smart 87 minutes), Hyde, Mooney, Johnson, Wright (Hazan 87 minutes).

Subs Not Used: Day. • **Booked:** Palmer, Kennedy, Ngonge, Gibbs, Smart. • **Attendance:** 29,100 • **Ref:** D Pugh (Wirral).
• **Aggregate:** 1–1 Watford won 7–6 on penalties

Match Report:

Watford are just 90 minutes from a return to the top flight for the first time in eleven years after reaching the Play-off Final in the most heart-breaking fashion. Hornet's manager Graham Taylor is now just a Wembley show-down against Bolton Wanderers away from masterminding the seventh promotion of his career and the second in successive seasons. But after 120 nerve-wracking minutes, it eventually took 16 penalties to decide the tie with Watford 'keeper Alec Chamberlain the hero and City midfielder Chris Holland – number 13 after 13 successful spot-kicks – the lonely, for-lorn figure.

Taylor had gone into this game having prepared meticulously as his side had practised spot-kicks at the end of their practice sessions since Sunday's first leg.

Watford were protecting a slender 1–0 advantage afforded to them by former Zaire international Michel Ngonge in the first leg at Vicarage Road.

But that lead was wiped out after just 110 seconds as fellow African Dele Adebola, Birmingham's giant Nigerian striker, levelled the aggregate scores on the night.

Adebola was in the starting line-up for the first time in six matches following a series of niggly injuries and despite not being 100% fit. But as City boss Trevor Francis was determined to go gunning for glory, so it ensured the 23-year-old forward was in the starting line up from the first whistle.

He made an instant impact, plundering his 17th goal of the season, but probably the most bizarre of his career. As Watford attempted to clear a second minute corner, the ball fell to Bryan Hughes who pumped a header back into the danger zone.

Peter Ndlovu looped a chance over the advancing defence and Chamberlain, only to see the ball strike the left hand post.

As the ball trickled across the goal line Watford centre-back Steve Palmer attempted to clear, but he only succeeded in striking the hulking figure of Adebola – but more importantly his elbow. However, the lack of ideas from both sides, not least because of the nerves and the tension, lead to a turgid stalemate until 10 minutes from the end of normal time. There was a flurry of yellow cards, including a red for Birmingham centre-back David Holdsworth, as City desperately strove for the game winner.

But they were denied by the outstanding Chamberlain who pulled off several outstanding stops, as well as two in injury time, to finally send the game into the dreaded penalty shoot-out.

After Peter Kennedy had blazed home the first, former Watford striker Paul Furlong saw his effort saved by Chamberlain. But the situation was levelled with the very next 12-yarder as Watford's Steve Palmer struck his effort wide. The next 12 penalties all found their target, with Richard Johnson, Darren Bazeley, Micah Hyde, Robert Page, Allan Smart and Alon Hazan all finding the net for Watford.

While for the Blues, Martin Grainger, Gary Rowett, Lee Bradbury, Hughes, Darren Purse, and even 'keeper Kevin Poole were the heroes for the home side.

But then it came down to poor Holland, whose right foot effort lacked any power, allowing Chamberlain to save with ease and to spark emotions on both sides of the fence. For Birmingham there were tears of sadness and heads in hands, while for Watford it was tears of joy and heads held high.

While Watford boss Taylor can go on to a Wembley Final with Bolton, for Birmingham boss Francis he now faces the most important decision of his career.

After an illustrious playing career at club and international level, and following three years in charge at St Andrews, Francis may decide that this is the end of the road for him. His 12 months rolling contract is again up for renewal, but a lot will depend on just how much money he is given by the City board to spend on transfers in a bid to end Birmingham's 13-year exile outside the top flight.

MEMORABLE GAME 4

BOLTON 0 – WATFORD 2 • 31 May 1999

Nationwide First Division Play-off Final

Bolton: Steve Banks, Neil Cox, Robbie Elliott, Per Frandsen, Andy Todd, Mark Fish (Captain), Michael Johansen, Claus Jensen, Eidur Gudjohnsen, Bob Taylor, Ricardo Gardner.

Substitutes: Bo Hansen for Neil Cox (89 minutes), Scott Sellars for Michael Johansen (66 minutes), Gudni Bergsson.
Manager: Colin Todd.

Watford: Alec Chamberlain, Darren Bazeley, Peter Kennedy, Robert Page (Captain), Steve Palmer, Paul Robinson, Michel Ngonge, Micah Hyde, Tommy Mooney, Richard Johnson, Nick Wright.

Substitutes: Allan Smart for Michel Ngonge (75 minutes) Alon Hazan for Nick Wright (87 minutes).
Scorers: Wright 38 minutes Smart 89 minutes.
Manager: Graham Taylor.
Bookings: Robbie Elliott (Bolton) Micah (Watford).
Wembley Stadium Attendance: 70,343 Referee Terry Heilbron

Paul was asked in a newspaper article, 'What does Wembley mean to you?' he replied:

'It's been quite a 12 months for me – I've become a first-team regular, been called into the England Under-21 squad and now I am here in the Play-off Final at Wembley.'

I could not ask for anything more. My dream as a boy was to be a professional footballer, and the things that have happened to me since then are
unbelievable. People still ask me about the old Wembley from when I won
there in the Play-offs with Watford and to be honest I preferred that mainly
because of the long walk out onto the pitch. I wish they had kept that walk
and the twin towers, the tradition has been taken away.

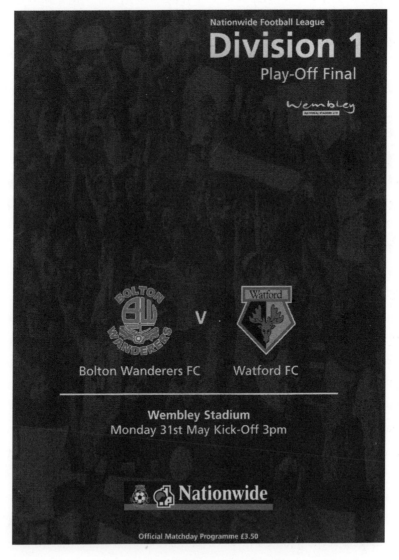

Championship Play-Off Programme

Celebrating at Wembley – Cairan Cosgrave front row left?

Match Report:

'So we can believe in fairy tales' wrote Brian Woolnough of *The Sun* – 'life has come full circle for Graham Taylor. Good Luck to him. As England manager he went to hell and back and now he is in heaven again. How fantastic for Taylor that one of the great moments in his career should be at Wembley where he suffered so much with England. After one disappointing result, he sang, "Oh Misery, misery, what's to become of me?" (a line from the Buddy Holly song *Raining in My Heart*.)

'Well Graham after goals from Nick Wright and Allan Smart, you are going to the Premiership, that's what. Taylor, Elton John and Watford in the Premiership! They have done it again, an incredible, amazing achievement. Taylor took Watford from the old Fourth Division to the First Division and into Europe via the FA Cup Final in the early 80s. Off he went on his travels to Aston Villa, England and Wolves before returning home to Vicarage Road. He was back with his family, and boy did they appreciate him yesterday after this latest Play-off Final drama. At the final whistle Taylor was mobbed by his staff, players and every emotion this wonderful sport offers us. At that moment, no doubt he would have loved to have waved two fingers at the people who have haunted, chased and criticised him for so long. But not a bit of it. There was only dignity from Taylor. It was meant to be and I suspect, deep down, felt that before the start. His close friend Elton John watched live from Seattle where he is on tour. Football must never give up these fairy tale moments. We know the biggest are getting bigger, but Watford and Bradford, who join them in the Premiership carry the flag for the minnows. You had to be at Wembley seeing the pure joy on the faces of the Hornets fans, to know it is so vital that football is not dominated by money alone.

'Watford know they will probably struggle next season. But this is their moment, and Taylor's moment, and they must be allowed to accept and enjoy it. No doubt Manchester United, Arsenal and Chelsea will be rubbing their hands at the prospect of easy pickings. That will not concern Watford at the moment and, one thing is certain, you should never underestimate Taylor. He has shown great character to fight off that past, plus serious illness this season, to produce one of the great modern-day stories. There is no question that Watford deserved their victory. It was not a fantastic football match, neither was it sophisticated, but Taylor's team emerged the stronger and better outfit. They had heroes in vital positions.

'When Bolton threatened in the first-half, goalkeeper Alec Chamberlain made two superb saves. His acrobatic reaction to palm away Eidur Gudjohnsen's volley was magnificent, one of the saves of the season. Gudjohnsen had earlier missed a sitter, sliding the ball wide when it seemed easier to score. That was the story of Bolton's defeat. In front of Chamberlain,

'Steve Palmer and Robert Page stood firm. Michael Owen, Dennis Bergkamp and Dwight Yorke will not have it all their own way against these two next season. And then there was the match-winner – 24-year-old Wright. He was picked up for £100,000 from Carlisle a year ago and ran this game with the swagger and dribbling control of Steve McManaman. He went past Robbie Elliott with ease and only came off with three minutes to go because he was knackered. It was Wright who fittingly broke the deadlock. A 37th minute corner from Peter Kennedy was headed up and out by Andy Todd. But not far enough – and Wright hooked it back over his right shoulder with a spectacular overhead kick. As the ball dropped in, Taylor sprung off his seat and punched the air in delight. In Seattle John shed another tear. Watford held firm when Bolton staged a brief counter at the start of the second half. But they were not meant to score; it simply was not in this script. Taylor's team should have put their manager out of his misery long before their second goal. Micah Hyde, another impressive performer, crossed from the right and Tommy Mooney's header grazed a post. Wright just failed to connect with Mooney's cross and then Kennedy drove wide when Wright put him clear. Gudjohnsen had Watford worried when his shot squeezed wide of Chamberlain and ran across the line. Moments later Watford scored again. Bolton sub Scott Sellars was robbed in midfield by Hyde, who pushed the ball out to the overlapping Kennedy. The cross was perfect; the first time shot by substitute Smart even better. Taylor called it the greatest day of his life. How he has waited for this. It is a fairy-tale. Just another fantastic football fairy-tale.

How They Rated – Watford

Alec Chamberlain – The golden oldie rolled back the years to produce one brilliant stop form Eidur Gudjohnsen and the keeper rarely looked troubled. 7/10

Darren Bazeley – Another Hornet stalwart who showed strength at the back and a keenness to go forward. 7/10

Peter Kennedy – Takes the corners and free-kicks but still has time for dangerous runs from the left. Laid on Watford's second goal. 8/10

Robert Page – The skipper can set off for Wales duty knowing that he kept Bob Taylor in his pocket all afternoon. 8/10

Steve Palmer – Hero defender who made sure that Bolton's free-scoring hit men got few strikes at goal. 7/10

Paul Robinson – Big, brave and a battering ram who gave Bolton's forwards few chances. 7/10

Michel Ngonge – Always dangerous with his runs and looked like scoring only to be denied by Elliott. 7/10

Micah Hyde – Stunning display from the midfielder, who seemed to be everywhere at once. Started the move for the second goal. 8/10

Tommy Mooney – Goal hero of recent weeks might not have found the net but he still caused Bolton plenty of problems and saw one header go just wide. 7/10

Richard Johnson – Holding well in midfield and provided valuable back-up for the defence. 7/10

Nick Wright – The hero of the moment. His brilliant overhead kick put Watford ahead. 9/10

Substitutes: Alon Hazan – Did his job well. 6/10, **Allan Smart** – Took killer goal superbly. 7/10

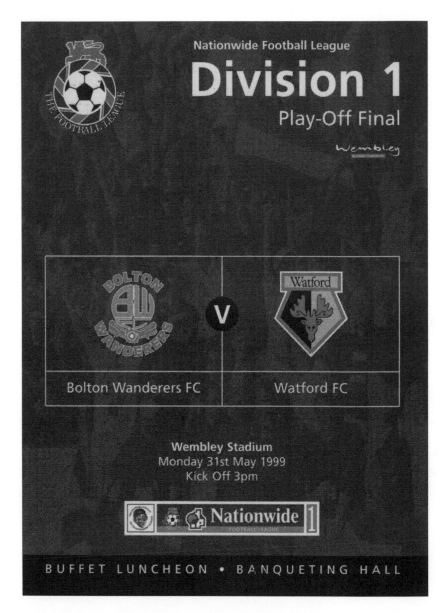

Play Off Final Hospitality Menu Cover

Play Off Final Hospitality Menu

MEMORABLE GAME 5

LIVERPOOL 0 – WATFORD 1

Saturday 14 August 1999 will always be a significant date in Paul's professional career as he rates the Hornets 1–0 defeat of Liverpool at Anfield to be the best game of his career.

Newly promoted Watford underlined Liverpool's defensive frailties again as they pulled off a shock victory at Anfield.

Tommy Mooney got the only goal in the 14th minute as he punished sloppiness at the back by side-footing home. It gave former England boss Taylor his first ever points at Anfield in 22 years as a manager and his first victory since returning to the top flight. Liverpool were not short of chances but they could not find a breakthrough. New Anfield skipper Jamie Redknapp worked hard at the heart of a midfield, which strove to provide a service on which revitalised striker Robbie Fowler could thrive.

But it was always a frustrating blend of quality and vulnerability from the new Anfield foreign legion, which lacked cohesion. Taylor had spent not a penny in the summer, in stark contrast to Liverpool boss Gerard Houllier's £25m of expenditure.

Liverpool were without £8m midfield signing Dietmar Hamann and injured Michael Owen, who hopes to return to full training next week. Torrential rain also made things difficult but there were too many holes in Liverpool's defence for comfort.

In the 16th minute Watford defender Peter Kennedy clipped in a free-kick which skidded about the Anfield penalty area like a pinball before landing at the feet of Mooney. The Watford striker could hardly believe the space he had found in an otherwise crowded penalty box.

He gratefully side-footed the ball beyond Dutch goalkeeper Sander Westerveld, before being submerged in a euphoric sea of yellow jerseys. Liverpool should have hauled themselves level before half-time with Steven Gerrard, Redknapp and Berger all squandering gilt-edged opportunities. But there was too much panic about Liverpool and the Anfield crowd's mood was quickly changing from optimism to exasperation.

In the 58th minute Houllier threw on David Thompson to replace Gerrard. Fowler immediately came close twice with a header and then a shot, which struck defender Paul Robinson.

But the more Liverpool pushed forward the more vulnerable they looked at the back and Watford should have increased their lead in the 81st minute. Mooney shot against the legs of goalkeeper Westerveld on the edge of the area and then Micah Hyde's chip was headed off the line by Liverpool substitute Rigobert Song.

Watford had further opportunities to increase Liverpool's embarrassment, with Mooney and Noel-Williams again going close. But the single goal was enough to provoke a party among the travelling fans from Hertfordshire.

Liverpool: Westerveld, Matteo, Hyypia, Carragher, Heggem, Berger, Redknapp, Gerrard, Smicer, Fowler, Camara.
Substitutes: Song, Staunton, Riedle, Friedel, Thompson.

Watford: Day, Lyttle, Kennedy, Palmer, Page, Robinson, Ngonge, Hyde, Mooney, Johnson, Williams.
Substitutes: Easton, Gudmundsson, Bonnot, Foley.

Referee: A Wilkie (Chester-le-Street)

The Sunday People statistics:

Statistic	Liverpool	Watford
Goal Attempts	22	13
Offsides	1	3
Corners	9	3
Free Kicks Conceded	8	8

Fouls Committed	7	7
Yellow Cards	1	2
Red Cards	0	0

The Sunday People **Watford Player Ratings**

Player	Comment	Score out of 10
DAY	Man of the Match – a perfect day	8
LYTTLE	Plenty of heart	6
WILLIAMS	Had his hands full	6
PAGE	At full stretch	6
ROBINSON	Fought his corner	7
HYDE	Did not hide	6
PALMER	Willing workhorse	7
JOHNSON	Cruelly injured (EASTON –Sub)	7 (6)
KENNEDY	Top left foot	7
MOONEY	Over the moon	7
NGONGE	Agile and athletic	7

MEMORABLE GAME 6

SOUTHAMPTON 2 – WATFORD 1 • 13 April 2003

Venue: Villa Park, Birmingham FA Cup semi-final

Watford: Alec Chamberlain, Neil Cox, Marcus Gayle, Paul Robinson, Neal Ardley, Micah Hyde, Stephen Glass, Paolo Vernazza, Gavin Mohan, Heidar Helguson, Michael Chopra.
Scorer: Marcus Gayle 88 minutes.
Yellow Cards: Neil Cox (31 minutes), Paul Robinson (57 minutes) and Heidar Helguson (70 minutes).
Substitutes: Allan Nielsen for Paolo Vernazza (56 minutes), Tommy Smith for Michael Chopra (70 minutes) and Lee Cook for Stephen Glass (77 minutes). Unused: Sean Dyche and Richard Lee.

Southampton: Paul Jones, Claus Lundekvam. Michael Svensson, Wayne Bridge, Matt Oakley, Paul Telfer, Chris Marsden, Anders Svensson, Fabrice Fernades, Brett Ormerod, James Beattie.
Scorers: Brett Ormerod 43 minutes, Paul Robinson (own goal) 80 minutes.
Yellow Cards: Fabrice Fernades (72 minutes).
Substitutes: Rory Delap for Anders Svensson (78 minutes) and Jo Tessem for Brett Ormerod (90 minutes). Unused: Kevin Davies, Danny Higginbotham and Alan Blayney.

Attendance: 42602 • **Referee:** Mike Riley.

Match Report:

Southampton have far more than a journey to Cardiff for the final to look forward to after this victory. Next season Europe beckons. With Arsenal heading for the Champions League, Gordon Strachan's team will claim the

UEFA place on offer for this competition even if they are beaten by the holders at the Millennium Stadium next month. Today Watford, tomorrow the world.

Almost 20 years have passed since Southampton last competed in Europe, in the 1984–85 season, but the strides taken by the club under Strachan have guaranteed an exciting reward after the summer. Perhaps they will be FA Cup winners by then, too. They have beaten Arsenal once already this season, winning 3–2 at St Mary's in November.

Southampton will surely have to improve on this display to defeat Arsène Wenger's team, but that can wait. A Brett Ormerod header and a Paul Robinson own-goal earned them a win they just about deserved yesterday in a scrappy yet passionate encounter. Marcus Gayle's late header provided Watford hope and gave the score line a fairer reflection but the First Division side lacked the quality to complement their endeavour.

Though the game was hardly a classic, it was poised neatly enough to hold the attention. Southampton never found life easy against opponents who set out to deny them fluency by closing down quickly but overall they had the edge. There were periods when Watford caused them problems, notably at the start of the second half, but Paul Jones pulled off an impressive and important stop at 1–0 to help Southampton on their way.

In Ormerod, Strachan had a striker who found his scoring touch at an ideal moment. The former Blackpool player had gone 23 games and almost six months without a goal before this match, last finding the net at home to Fulham on 27 October. Here he scored before half-time to cap his team's best spell, also setting up the second when Robinson touched his cross over the line as James Beattie slid in.

Beattie celebrated after the game in a ginger wig worn by Southampton fans as a tribute to Strachan. It should not be forgotten that the club were 19th in the Premiership when the Scot replaced Stuart Gray in October 2001. They may have faced only one top-flight club, Tottenham, en route to this final but they demolished Spurs in the third round and avoided slip-ups against four successive First Division clubs.

This victory was professional rather than spectacular. Jones, replacing the injured Antti Niemi for his first appearance since December, made a vital early stop. The central midfielders, Matt Oakley and Anders Svensson, made sure their work rate matched Watford's efforts. Ormerod was always willing and used the ball well, while Beattie never stopped running. A couple of tackles deep in his own half confirmed he offers more than goals.

Watford, as expected, were equally tireless. There were moments when their play was neat but high energy was the basis of their efforts. They enjoyed their most productive period when Neal Ardley was sending over crosses from the right flank. Stephen Glass met one with a far-post header that Jones did well to keep out via the bar.

Heidar Helguson and Michael Chopra, the striker on loan from Newcastle, never seriously threatened to get behind a Southampton defence well marshalled by Claus Lundekvam, but Watford had other openings. Chopra saw a shot well blocked by Wayne Bridge and Micah Hyde might have done better with a shot that was deflected wide.

By chasing hard from the strikers back, Watford forced Southampton to play more long balls than they would have liked in the first half. Even if Beattie won flick-ons, there was no one running on to them, and Southampton's best moments before the interval tended to come via Fabrice Fernandes on the right or when Bridge made overlapping runs on the left.

The breakthrough came when Anders Svensson won a challenge in midfield and fed Chris Marsden, whose cross was met unmarked by Ormerod. Chamberlain got a glove on the ball but, unlike David Seaman in the earlier semi-final, could not keep it out. It was Watford's first conceded goal in this Cup run.

After Michael Svensson had wasted a free header for Southampton and Watford had wasted a couple of chances, Ormerod set up the decisive strike. Again Watford lost the ball in midfield, this time Hyde being dispossessed by the substitute Rory Delap, Ormerod accelerated and centred, and Robinson got the final touch.

When Gayle got ahead of Beattie and headed in an Ardley corner, Watford sensed a way back. But it was not to be. They are left with a sense of disappointment but also fond memories of a fine Cup run. Southampton have not just the Final but Europe to fill their minds.

Although I was never a captain at Vicarage Road I learned a lot and gained inspiration to be a captain in the future from Robert Page. He was a Welsh International, playing 41 times for his country over ten years; because of his club captaincy qualities he was given the national arm band on one occasion. He began his career at Watford in 1993 and he captained the side to its two successive promotions in 1998 and 1999 thereby securing the club a place in the top-flight of English Football leaving in 2001.

So there I was at the age of 24 moving from my hometown club to The Hawthorns for £250,000 and I immediately set my sights on the top flight. Despite my strong connections at Vicarage Road, the lure of potential Premiership football at Albion was too strong to turn down. The move came out of the blue – I didn't have a clue West Bromwich Albion were even interested. I'd been at Watford all of my career, so when the club agreed to sell me I had a hard decision to make, not just for me but for my wife and young son. When I left Watford in October 2003 I left with fond memories, I had enjoyed every moment of my time at Watford. To be a local lad that came through the ranks and played first team football for my local club was brilliant. I loved every bit of it and really enjoyed my football.

When I first went back to Vicarage Road with the Albion, the fans reaction to me was fantastic. I didn't get a chance to say goodbye as the move was done in quite a short space of time when I left, that was a shame, as I would have liked to have said thanks to everyone, not least the fans who were absolutely brilliant to me when I was up and coming and then playing in the first team so it was a great chance for me to send my regards to everyone and thank everyone for their support. The welcome I got was unbelievable and definitely a moment to treasure and I will always remember it. I had goose bumps and the hairs were standing up on the back of my neck. People were clapping and shouting Robbo. I didn't expect it. I always thought I would get a nice reception, but what I got was unbelievable and I was overwhelmed.

The Watford fans felt great affection for Robbo and also felt they did not get the chance to say goodbye properly. This resulted in the following:

Frances Lynn wrote in the Watford FC fanzine *Look At The Stars*, Issue Sixteen Christmas 2003 an article entitled 'Auf Wiedersehen, Robbo'.

There is sometimes a defining moment when a player changes from being a golden-shirted hero into a real human being. I had always appreciated Robbo for his passion and his tour of the stands at the end of the game. And on my visits to #vicarage_road on IRC I would stick up for him against those 'internet' fans that would seek to question his contribution. But I have to admit that his 'red-mist' moments often brought out the middle-aged woman in me, tut tutting at the young boy's over exuberance, and the cynic in me would question the self-indulgence, then came my defining moment. It was at the Sponsor's Evening two days after the FA Cup semi-final defeat. My sister Cate (a bone fide Robbo fan) and I encountered him with the question that we had posed to all the players, 'How are you feeling after Sunday?' Robbo just went off on one. 'HE FOULED ME FOR THE GOAL. I WOULD HAVE CLEARED IT IF HE HADN'T FOULED ME. AND THAT WAS NEVER A YEL-LOW CARD … HE DIVED. EVEN STRACHAN WAS SHOUT-ING AT HIM FOR DIVING, AND NOW I'LL MISS THE END OF THE SEASON AND THE START OF NEXT SEASON.'

He was as distraught as any fan I had spoken to and, more than that, the tone of his distress made it clear that he was as concerned that we, the fans, would feel that he had let us down. Cate and I turned into two mother hens. 'It's all right, Robbo. No one is blaming you. There was nothing you could have done.' And in that instant he had changed in my perception from being a psychotic hard man to a nice young lad.

Then a mere six months later, the hideous rumour started. West Bromwich Albion had put in a surprise bid for Robbo, and the Board was going to accept it. There was a sense of disbelief and then a horrible realisation of how poverty-stricken our beloved club is at the moment. And then he was gone.

My cousin is an Arsenal fan and to hear her talk about the youngsters e.g. Ashley Cole, that left her beloved club for 'better things' brings home the increasingly fickle nature of today's professional. Cole suddenly declared himself a lifelong Chelsea fan – what a contrast that attitude is to that of Robbo who gave a heart-wrenching interview with Watford World. This lad had been with the club since he was nine years old, well over half his life, and he obviously loved the place. The way his voice cracked when he said that Watford was like a second family to him was enough to break the hardest heart. And his expressed desire to come back and finish his career at Vicarage Road was not the sort of thing that is usually said under these circumstances and was utterly believable.

I still get a start when I see him on the highlights show wearing a Tesco carrier bag. And I live in hope that it is 'auf wiedersehen' and 'au revoir' and NOT 'goodbye Robbo'.

When he left Vicarage Road Robbo was given a black notebook from the fans, which includes 338 farewell messages from Hornets fans, a fantastic testament to the popularity of ROBBO.

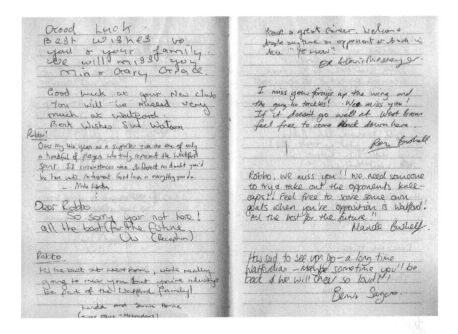

Robbo's Little Black Book

Here is a small sample of the good wishes he received:

'Paul, I've seen you both at school and at Watford – what a great kid and a true professional! All the best Eugene O'Reilly (St Micks) P.S. John Ridgewell sends his best.'

'Dear Mr Robbo You still are my daughter's dreamboat. She was the mascot for last season's Gillingham game! No doubt our paths WILL cross again, you are the proverbial "stick of rock" – Watford through and through Never to be forgotten The Stanton Family.'

'All the best Robbo You leave us with many memories of your 50/50 tackles and your ventures up the left wing … And your goal against L***N Beezer.'

'THERE WAS A YOUNG MAN PLAYED LEFT-BACK

BUT HE OFTEN PREFERRED TO ATTACK

SOME THINK HE'S A YOBBO

BUT WE LOVE YOU ROBBO

AND HOPE THAT ONE DAY YOU'LL COME BACK!'

With love Kathryn and Tim Maynard

And last but not least

'Dear Robbo

You have been my favourite player for seven years, and I am so upset that you have left. But of course I wish you all the luck in the world and hope you do well at West Brom and that you and your family are happy, which is the most important thing. Although Watford will always be number one in my heart, already it is not the same without you here. Thank you for all the loyalty, spirit, passion and commitment you have given over the years, it was always 110% and that is why we will all miss you. Good Luck again for the future, as far as I am concerned, the number three shirt at Watford will always belong to you. You are a golden boy through and through and I can't wait until you come back. We miss you! Lots of Love Vanessa.'

Paul also received a letter from Kenny Jackett, now manager of Wolverhampton Wanderers:

Dear Paul,

Just a quick note to wish Caroline, Luke and yourself the very best of luck in the Midlands, we hope it goes well. West Bromwich was an excellent move for you Paul, there comes a time in your playing career when you need to move on and the time was right for yourself. I am sure that it will be tough establishing yourself at a new club and settling in a new area but you are easily good enough to do it and I am sure it will make you a better player and a person. Anyway I will be following your fortunes. All the best for the remainder of the season and keep working hard.

Regards Ken.

I still keep in touch with Tommy Smith who went through the same experiences as me at Vicarage Road. I spoke to him before he went back to Watford to play for a second time in 2006, and he was worried how people would react to him going back. I had no doubt he would go back there and do a fantastic job and he did exactly that, making 124 appearances and scoring 27 goals before he left in 2009.

'Smudger' was born on 22 May 1980 in Hemel Hempstead, Hertfordshire not far from Watford so it was no surprise that he started his career at Watford, where his younger brother Jack was also a trainee. Like me he played a part in Watford's consecutive promotions and it's relegation in 2000. Again like me, he represented his country at under 21 level the following season. During the period 1997–2003 he made 149 appearances scoring 33 goals before joining Sunderland on a free transfer in 2003. His subsequent performances earned him consecutive Watford Player of the Season awards in 2007–08 and 2008–09. At the start of the following season he was sold to Premier League club Portsmouth. His father Dave, a chartered surveyor and former Watford youth team player, helped coach with the academy during his son's time there. Tommy has been with his wife Nina since leaving school. They married in 2005 have three children.

Outside of football, Smith's interests include golf and films. In 2014 he and his brother Jack took over the sales arm of an estate agent and chartered surveyors.

Other ex-Watford players I keep in touch with are Wardy; I speak to him every now and then. Richard Lee I speak to, Lloyd Doyley I keep in touch with. All the other lads from our era have moved on in different directions now.

At Watford I got my first taste of the Premiership and I was able to experience how big the difference was for a full-back from playing Championship football and Premiership football. The difference can be enormous if you are trying to mark Ronaldo! I just go into every game with the intention of playing as well as I can but at this level you are playing against world-class players who are fully fledged internationals. They are fitter and stronger but you have to enjoy these moments. It was a challenge for me but one I enjoy.

Even from the last time I was in the Premiership with West Bromwich Albion and before that with Watford, the difference from then to now is huge. The players are just so good. In the Championship you get more physical wingers who will try and bully you more and rough you up. With people knowing what I am like, they try and wind me up to try and get a reaction and try to get me to throw a punch at someone, where as in the Premier league the wingers will try and run at you and see what you are like as a defender. It's not in my mind to think about kicking players up in the air, however if there is a tackle there to be won then I will go in for it. If I catch people afterwards then I will pick them up and apologise.

You will read later in the book my opinions on the loan system but the death of a loanee at Watford was a very sad event to say the least.

James Roger William 'Jimmy' Davis
(6 February 1982 – 9 August 2003) – R.I.P.

Jimmy was on loan to Watford from Manchester United at the time of his death after spending loan periods in Belgium with Royal Antwerp and Swindon Town, bizarrely Jimmy never did make a senior appearance for Manchester United. I was playing golf with him the week before he died.

He was killed in a car crash on the M40 motorway in the early hours of 9 August 2003. He crashed his BMW into a truck and was pronounced dead at the scene. The truck driver suffered minor injuries. The accident occurred just hours before Watford were due to open their season with a match against Coventry City. The Watford board of directors announced later that morning that the match was postponed due to 'tragic circumstances beyond their control', though they did not announce Davis' death for another few hours. His funeral took place at Redditch Crematorium, with the Manchester United team in attendance.

The subsequent inquest reported that Davis was more than twice over the legal drink-drive limit and it was believed that he had been driving at speeds of up to 120 mph when losing control of his car when he fell asleep at the wheel. The inquest returned a verdict of accidental death. The loss rocked football and perhaps was a message that success at a young age can have its tragic downsides.

'We called all the players into the dressing room and broke the news,' Ray Lewington, the then Watford manager, said. 'Paul took it the worst. He broke down straight away.'

Goal celebration with Ray Lewington

In the ALBION match day magazine against Watford on 31 January 2004 Ray Lewington was quoted:

> 'We've got no money, up until a couple of weeks back we couldn't even look at loans really, though the money we made from the Cup eased that. But it's tight, we run with what we've got but I've known that since I came in. It does make it tough, like when we lost Paul Robinson to you. Our Chairman phoned me up and said "I've got some bad news for you, West Brom have made us an offer for Paul and we've got to take it". What made it worse was he was our only natural left-back, they're at a premium, and as you've seen by now, he's a good lad, decent attitude, nice left peg, works hard and losing him was a blow.'

Nigel Gibbs, a former teammate at Watford, recalls an incident that provides a snapshot of Robinson's character.

'I had taken his place in the [1999] Play-off semi-final at Birmingham [as Robinson was suspended] but I was left out at Wembley for the Final against Bolton and was not even on the bench,' Gibbs, who is now assistant coach at Reading, said. 'He recognised that and gave me his spare shirt after the game which was a lovely gesture.'

Robinson is also something of a character in the dressing room.

'We had a running machine fitted and you had to be careful of those,' Lewington said.

'Well, Paul was always game for a laugh and he put the machine on full speed and said that he could jump on it and stay on it. He jumped on but the thing catapulted him backwards and he ended up in as heap, cutting his chin in the process.'

Watford's Paul Robinson imitates Leeds United's
Robbie Keane's trademark goal celebration

The table below shows my season by season appearances for the Vicarage Road club:

SEASON	LEAGUE	FA CUP	LEAGUE CUP	OTHER	TOTAL
1996–97	12(0)	3(0)	0(0)	2(0)	17(0)
1997–98	22(2)	2(0)	0(0)	1(0)	25(2)
1998–99	29(0)	1(0)	2(0)	2(0)	34(0)
1999–2000	32(0)				32(0)
2000–01	39(0)	1(0)	4(0)	0(0)	44(0)
2001–02	38(3)	0(0)	5(1)	0(0)	43(4)
2002–03	37(3)	4(0)	1(0)	0(0)	42(3)
2003–04	10(0)	0(0)	1(0)	0(0)	11(0)
TOTAL	219(8)	11(0)	16(1)	5(0)	248(9)

4.

'West Bromwich Albion'

In October 2003 Robinson was sold to West Bromwich Albion for an initial £250,000 fee, potentially rising to £375,000 depending on appearances and Albion being promoted to the Premiership. He made his West Bromwich Albion debut in a 1–0 win against Norwich City on 18 October 2003.

Upon his arrival at The Hawthorns he was reported as saying:

'But I'm an ambitious person and when a club like West Bromwich Albion come in for you there really is no choice – you can't turn that kind of challenge down. 'I'm now looking to settle down, although finding a place to live in the Midlands has taken longer than I thought. I wanted to have a good look around and find somewhere where my family would be happy, but fingers crossed we've now found that.

'It's something I'm looking to change because I picked up 15 yellow cards and a red last season and spent far too long on the side lines,' he said. 'I've always been a fully committed player and I won't be ducking out of any challenges. But I'm looking to stay on my feet more because if you keep picking up bookings you're letting yourself, the manager, team-mates and fans down.

'At Watford I was first choice and straight in the side every week, but that's not the case at Albion, You have to fight for every position here and that should be the kind of challenge that will improve me as a player. My form has been getting better every week as I get to know the rest of the team, and I'm really enjoying getting the chance to play at The Hawthorns. At Watford we used to get crowds of 12,000 but at Albion you get double that which can take some getting used to.

'I am hoping that my move from the foot of Division One to pro-motion chasing Albion will not only take me back to the promised land of the Premiership but also kick-start my fledgling inter-national career. Everyone who plays professional football would love to play for their country, and I'm no different, to play for the England Under-21 team was a great achievement and moving to a bigger club like Albion has obviously boosted my chances of yet more honours. But for the moment my main priority this season is getting back into the Premiership and staying there.

'I have Gary Megson (Note: From March 2000 to October 2004 Played 221 Won 94 Drew 50 Lost 77 Win Ratio 42.53%) to thank for giving me my Hawthorns' chance.

I'll always be in debt to him. Gary brought me here and gave me my chance at a massive club. He's moved on because football evolves. He's at Bolton now and it'll be nice to catch up with him – mind you I'm sure I won't get as much earache as his own players! We've all seen what Gary's like. He doesn't need to do one-on-ones; he'll bawl you out on the pitch in 11 v 11. Players need those wake-up calls sometimes for their concentration. I never had any run-ins with him but I do think you need a certain personality to be able to work with managers like that. Managers have to accept that some players are fiery and may not be afraid to say something them-selves. That's the great thing about football. Sometimes instead of hiding you can bring it out into the open.

'Megson and Tony Mowbray (Note: From October 2006 to June 2009 Played 148 Won 57 Drew 32 Lost 51 Win Ratio 40.71%) are complete opposites. I enjoyed working for Gary and the way that he enjoyed football. The gaffer (Tony Mowbray) loses his temper now and then but, his philosophy is second to none.

'He likes us playing football and he gave us responsibility on the pitch. He's calm, collected and that reflects on the players. His football knowledge is unbelievable, and the way he got us to play football was just second to none. It was really enjoyable working for him.'

After Gary left Frank Burrows was appointed caretaker manager for two games in the autumn of 2004 before the appointment of Bryan Robson with Nigel Pearson as his assistant. (Note: From November 2004 to September 2006 Played 81 Won 19 Drew 24 Lost 38 Win Ratio 23.46%)

Before he joined The Baggies Robson was convinced that Neil Clement would be his left-back but once he had seen everyone play he eventually switched Clement to centre-half and installed Robbo at left back. Robson explained his thinking, saying, 'I put him on in front of Clement against Manchester United because I thought he could play in midfield and protect Neil Clement. I spoke to him the following Monday and he told me he would do anything, but he could not play in midfield. That was good because I asked all the players to be honest with me. It made a real quick decision for me because I knew he was uncomfortable in midfield – I had to look at him as a left-back. He came in versus Manchester City for his first game after being out for a while and was outstanding in a really good defensive display from the team – he has gone on from there. When we do fitness tests he is right up there at the top – he is really fit. And I thought the way he whipped up the crowd on Sunday was brilliant.'

Robbo recalls, 'In April 2005 I renewed my contract with the Albion for a further two years with a further year's option in the club's favour. I was absolutely delighted to sign because in my own mind it was what I wanted. The family were settled and the lads at The Hawthorns had bonded well creating a great team spirit and I did not want to leave that. I had had to work hard to prove myself to Bryan Robson after failing to make the boss' first seven starting line-ups. As it happened it was for the best as I improved thanks to the Robson regime, because there was so much competition for places you could not relax. When Bryan first came in I couldn't get in the side but I worked hard, got my chance and consolidated my position in the starting line-up.'

In June 2006 Watford attempted to re-sign Robbo for £1.4m, however, this bid was rejected by manager Robson and Chairman Jeremy Peace, as he was considered vital if the team was to realise its ambition of a quick return to the Premier League. This resulted in Paul signing a new three-year contract with the club in July 2006.

But the interest in Paul did not cease, as he was the subject of a £1.5m bid from Premiership team Wigan Athletic in August 2007 as a replacement for Leighton Baines, who had been sold to Everton. The move fell through and was reported in the local press as follows:

The Express & Star reporter Steve Marshall ran a piece entitled 'ROBINSON SPELLS OUT HIS AIMS FOR BAGGIES.' Full-back reveals fitness fears were not reason for failed move.

Paul Robinson today spelled out his determination to put a turbulent summer behind him – and set his sights on helping Albion back to the Premiership.

Robinson found himself at the centre of a storm of transfer speculation over the summer as he was linked with moves to both Sunderland and Wigan Athletic. Neither move materialised amid rumours the tough tackling full-back had failed medicals, leaving his Premiership dreams in tatters. But speaking for the first time since the trail that appeared to have Robinson heading for the JJB

Stadium turned cold in August, the 28-year-old tells a very different story. Robinson claims the stories surrounding the state of his fitness were well wide of the mark and revealed the upset they caused for both him and his young family. He believes he is stronger for the experience and delighted he's back doing what he does best –playing football and terrorising opposition wingers.

'There was a lot of bad publicity that was blown out of proportion,' said Robinson. 'It was unnecessary. My track record proves I've never missed a game and some of the stories that came out put a downer on you. It makes you think there's something wrong with you when there's not. What people write is up to them but they have to think about the people involved and their family. My family supported me through it and I'm glad I'm back playing and enjoying my football, which is what I want to do. If anyone's been in that position where they've had stuff written about them that is not true then you always find it difficult. That's football and you have to deal with that. Thankfully I did. I'm lucky to have a fantastic wife and family who support me and the club has supported me as well. For me, it was just a case of getting back to doing what I love, which is playing football.'

One of the hardest things Robinson has to deal with was a question mark from some quarters over his commitment to the Baggies. And he pointed to the fact he took a succession of pain killing injections in the closing weeks of last season to try and help Albion's promotion push as proof of his desire for the club to succeed.

'That's just me and the type of person I am. It was upsetting when people were saying I'm not committed. People obviously don't know me if they're going to write in the paper that I am not committed. If they are going to say that they better think again because

I know for a fact that I put 110 percent into training and games. I put my head in where it hurts, that's just me as a person. And any suggestion I've had a fall-out with the manager is just rubbish. I can understand the fans' point of view from the stories that they read, but you have to deal with that. It was a tough time for me, but I've got over it. My team mates have supported me and that's been a great plus.'

In early November 2007 he was named in the Championship Team of the Week following Albion's 3–0 win at his former club Watford.

He made the Team of the Week once again after Albion's 4–3 home win against Colchester United in March 2008.

And then to top a great season Paul was named in the 2007–08 Football League Championship Professional Footballers' Association (PFA) Team of the Year, alongside team mates Jonathan Greening and Kevin Phillips after helping Albion win promotion to the Premiership as League Champions.

The full team was: Wayne Hennessey (Wolverhampton Wanderers), Bradley Orr (Bristol City), Ryan Shawcross (Stoke City), Danny Shittu (Watford), Paul Robinson (West Bromwich Albion), Liam Lawrence (Stoke City), Brian Howard (Barnsley), Marvin Elliott (Bristol City), Jonathan Greening (West Bromwich Albion), Ricardo Fuller (Stoke City) and Kevin Phillips (West Bromwich Albion).

Another goal celebration with KP – other players are Fillipe Texiara on the left and Robert Koran – that's Jonathan Greening's arm!

On August 27 2008 I signed a new two-year deal, with a 12-month option, at the time of signing my new contract I was Albion's second-longest serving player after Neil Clement.

West Bromwich Albion will appeal after Paul Robinson was controversially sent off in Tuesday's 5-0 defeat against Manchester United at The Hawthorns – 29 January 2009. Baggies boss Tony Mowbray said 'I've seen the sending off incident many times on the laptop in the dressing room. Mr Styles makes his decision. I can only comment from the angle I saw it initially. I didn't get Mr Styles' angle so I don't know what he saw. He thought it worthy of a red card and we have to abide by that for the time being. From the replays I've seen, it looked like a pretty committed challenge from two players. I would say they both sort of slid three or four yards from the ball and collided and hit knees together. Their player sort of crumpled up and the referee came striding over and brandished his red card. You'll have experts all over the telly giving their opinions, some saying it was a red card, some saying it was a disgrace and some saying it was never a red card. It's all about opinion and the referee made his decision tonight. From his angle he thought it was a red card. But if the TV angles show he didn't leave the ground, he didn't show his studs and it was just an honest collision between two players going for the ball, then I'm pretty sure there will be a case to appeal it.' The feisty left-back looked set to sit out the next three games after being harshly sent off against Manchester United by Rob Styles in the 40th minute on Tuesday night. However after the club appealed the decision to the FA, a disciplinary panel overturned Styles' decision to award a straight red-card for violent conduct on 29 January 2009.

> 'We're obviously delighted,' Tony Mowbray said after the decision was announced. 'It's a boost for everyone, particularly at this moment when we've lost our captain Jonathan Greening through injury. To lose our vice-captain as well would have been a big loss in terms of the character of the team. It's important we have leaders out there, personalities like his; Paul's a whole-hearted player. I see him tackling his own teammates like he did Ji-Sung Park on Tuesday every day in training. I sat in the dressing room after the game and watched the incident on the laptop. I couldn't see a sending-off, so I think it was right we appealed and I'm delighted it's been upheld.'

Had the card not been rescinded, the player would have been suspended for three matches. However the FA overturned the decision on appeal.

In March 2009 Paul criticised his team mates for failing to give their all for the club. The left-back who was relegated with Albion in 2006 said that some players needed to play with more 'pride and passion' if they are to survive this season. At that time Albion were anchored to the bottom of the league, four points adrift behind their nearest rivals, Middlesbrough, and six points from safety.

'It hurt last time we were relegated, because I know there was a bunch of players in there who worked their socks off, but there was another bunch of players who didn't, and I don't want it to happen again,' he said. 'As a group of players we have to sort that out and start producing. It has to be on the pitch and it has to be about results, and how to take this club forward. I want players to realise this is a fantastic club to be at. The supporters deserve more and as players we deserve more out of each other. There are a few out there who need to wear the shirt with a little more pride and passion, and commit themselves to this club a bit more. People have made mistakes and they have let it get to them and they have then gone missing for a bit. You can't afford to do that in the Premier League because you are letting your team-mates down.'

Paul continued this theme for survival with a further press report as follows:

'Paul Robinson has called on Tony Mowbray and Jeremy Peace to ensure that any January arrivals are willing to fight for Albion's survival cause. Robinson, who is a survivor of Albion's Great Escape in 2005 and is its longest serving player in the absence of injured Neil Clement. He feels this squad is better in terms of ability. But he believes that side had plenty of character, which is what Albion need to stand any chance of surviving. "It's about getting the right mixture to balance the squad off. But we've got to be careful to get the right players. We need people who want to come here and play for this club and not just want to come because of where we are playing. That's a decision that the gaffer and Chairman have got to make. They have to get players who they believe can help us, but at the same time can fit in with the squad and the club and are willing to play for the club and fight from the position were in. Whatever people write or say will be negative about what we're doing; we have come from worse positions than this. I think it was January or February and we had 10 points and we're better off than that now. We're not out of it by any means so we have to keep going into every game believing we can pick up three points."

'Paul Robinson hopes Kevin Phillips will remain at The Hawthorns – but accepts the 34-year-old will only do so if the terms are right. Phillips has yet to decide whether he will be signing a new deal at Albion or moving on. Albion are keen to keep Phillips but have yet to reach an agreement, with the player wanting a straight two-year deal. Robinson, one of Phillips' best friends at the club, is hopeful the matter will be resolved in Albion's favour. "It's up in the air at the moment but hopefully it will be sorted out," said Robinson. "He is a massive player for us and in the end his goals were probably the reason we got promoted last season. I know that Kev would like to stay. We are close friends and our families get on really well. But I know whatever Kev does will have to be right for him and his family. He scored 24 goals last season so I don't see a problem with his fitness. He is 34 years of age but he knows his own body better than anyone else and if he thinks he can play on in the Premier League that's good enough for me. All the lads want him to stay because he is a good character to have around the place and the younger lads can learn so much from him."'

Chairman Jeremy Peace has hinted West Bromwich Albion may be prepared to sell Paul Robinson, but only on their terms. Bolton are understood to have upped their bid to £750,000 having had a £500,000 offer rejected for the full-back, with Albion unwilling to let him go for anything less than £1million.

The Midlands outfit would prefer not to sell at all, but after the 30-year-old again expressed his desire to leave The Hawthorns, Peace admitted it could be something the club look into if a move benefits them.

Peace said: 'We have been here before with Paul. He has expressed his desire in the press to play elsewhere in no uncertain terms.' (Albion boss) Robbie (Di Matteo) (Note: From June 2009 to June 2011 Played 82 Won 40 Drew 29 Lost 23 Win Ratio 48.78%) has already spoken to him. Nobody is going to leave here unless they go with terms acceptable to us. 'If, on balance, it is felt a player is better off being elsewhere, then we would look at that.'

Note:

Jeremy Peace was born 13 August 1956 in West Bromwich and educated at Shrewsbury School. He worked in accountancy, stockbroking and in investment banking between 1974 and 1983. Until 1991, he was a major shareholder and director of Morland Securities PLC (later renamed Access Satellite International PLC) and then of Sangers Photographics PLC (later renamed Quadrant Group PLC).

Since that time, Peace has been a director and/or shareholder in various public limited companies namely South Country Homes, Thomas Potts, London Town, e-prime financial, EP&F Capital, Galahad Capital, Camelot Capital and West Bromwich Albion F.C.

Peace joined the board of West Bromwich Albion as a Non-Executive Director on December 8, 2000, and became Chairman in June 2002, following the resignation of Paul Thompson. The Company was taken private in 2005, with him owning a majority shareholding.

On May 31, 2013, Peace transferred his 59.9 percent shareholding in West Bromwich Albion Group Limited to a new company, West Bromwich Albion Holdings Limited. Peace is the sole director of West Bromwich Albion Holdings Limited and owns 100 per cent of the new company

In 2013, the *Daily Express* reported that Peace 'runs the club with a rod of iron. Any manager has to accept the title of "head coach" and be prepared to slot into the way Peace does things.'

I have played in some great games for West Bromwich Albion the details of which are documented here:

MEMORABLE GAME 7

ASTON VILLA 1 – WEST BROM ALBION 1 • 10 April 2005

Robbo's favourite goal throughout his career was a header against Aston Villa, which to Baggies fans was the 'Goal of The Season'.

Paul Robinson's header deep in injury time rescued a point for West Bromwich Albion to lift them out of the relegation zone

Goal against Aston Villa

Robinson struck at the far post to convert Riccardo Scimeca's cross. Darius Vassell had put Villa ahead, pouncing on a rebound after Russell Hoult superbly palmed Liam Ridgewell's header onto his crossbar. Both Hoult and Thomas Sorensen made good saves, while Ridgewell and Jonathan Greening both saw red for head-butting after the break. Albion with three wins from their previous four games, are now fourth-bottom in the Premiership and playing like a team who believe they can retain their Premiership status. But it seemed for so long as though Villa would take all the points to boost their flagging hopes of qualifying for European football next season. Villa went into the match on a sequence of win-one, lose-one that stretched back six games. And having defeated Newcastle United 3–0 last week, David O'Leary's team started at a bristling high-tempo, clearly determined to end their inconsistent run of form. Hoult bravely came off his line to smother Vassell's short-range strike, whilst Juan Pablo Angel headed wide and shot over. Samuel almost lobbed Hoult from a tight angle, but the Baggies 'keeper managed to turn the ball over his crossbar. From the subsequent corner Villa's committed start was rewarded with a goal. Ridgewell made a superb contact from Nolberto Solano's corner and Hoult did brilliantly to parry his header against the crossbar. Vassell was the first to pounce upon the rebound to put Villa in front. But with half-time looming the Baggies squandered two chances to equalise. Ronnie Wallwork delivered a precise far-post cross from the right but Kevin Campbell made a weak contact and his poorly directed header was easily saved. Then Laursen made a committed block to deflect a short-range shot from Campbell over after Richardson's deft flick had created the opening. West Bromwich Albion created another good chance shortly after the restart, Martin Albrechtsen's cross eluded Thomas Sorensen and Laursen bailed out his 'keeper, clearing at the second attempt with Geoff Horsfield lurking. Tensions rose when Ridgewell and Jonathan Greening clashed, locking heads and attempting to head-butt each other several times without seeming to make any meaningful contact. Both saw red for their foolish behaviour and the match swung back in Villa's favour, with Hoult brilliantly saving a Vassell header. But the Baggies refused to give up and Sorensen did well to save from Gera. West Bromwich Albion's tenacity was rewarded when Delaney inadvertently flicked Riccardo Scimeca's cross to the far post with Robinson pouncing to score his first goal for the club. David O'Leary the Aston Villa manager stated, 'I thought we should have wrapped it up in the first half and even though we were a shadow of ourselves in the second half, we should still have won the game.' Bryan Robson, Manager of the Albion said, 'It is only a point but it is the manner in which we got it which keeps the momentum going. The lads are in good form and really believe in themselves at the moment. It was important we got something out of the game. I was really pleased with the response in the second half. We competed really well, created some good situations and deserved a point.'

Aston Villa: Sorensen, Delaney, Laursen, Ridgewell, Samuel, Solano (De La Cruz 64 minutes), Hendrie, Davis, Barry, Angel (Cole 80 minutes) Vassell.
Unused Substitutes: Hitzlsperger, Postma and Berson.
Sent Off: Ridgewell (61 minutes). Booked Laursen.
Scorer: Vassell 27 minutes.

West Bromwich Albion: Hoult, Albrechtsen (Scimeca 80 minutes), Gaardsoe, Clement, Robinson, Gera, Wallwork, Richardson, Greening, Horsfield (Earnshaw 71 minutes), Campbell (Kanu 71 minutes).Unused Substitutes: Moore and Kuszczak. Sent Off Greening (61 minutes).
Booked: Robinson and Kanu.
Scorer: Robinson 90 minutes.

Attendance: 39,402 of which 3,750 were from The Albion
- **Referee:** R. Styles (Hampshire).

MEMORABLE GAME 8

WEST BROM ALBION 2 – PORTSMOUTH 0 • 15 May 2005

They billed it as the great escape, and in Premiership history there has been none greater. In last place at the start of play, West Bromwich Albion propelled themselves to a final position of fourth from bottom with a combination of victory over Portsmouth and a goal at The Valley by a man named Fortune.

Back Row: *Left to Right: Robert Earnshaw, Ronnie Wallwork, Riccardo Scimeca, Richard Chaplow and Kanu*
Front Row: *Left to Right: Andy Johnson, Neil Clement, Thomas Gaardsoe, Geoff Horsfield, Jonathan Greening, Robbo, Zoltan Gera, Bryan Robson and Darren Moore*

There was nothing fortunate about Albion's reprieve from relegation, which was secured by second-half goals from Geoff Horsfield and Kieran Richardson and will be worth £20m to the club. Since the élite division broke away in 1992, no team has survived after propping up the table at

Christmas. At that stage, a side still finding their way under a new manager, Bryan Robson, were eight points adrift of safety. The turning point was a last-gasp own-goal equaliser at Manchester City, a game in which Albion mustered neither a shot nor a header on target. Since New Year's Day, they have collected 24 points, the final three arriving yesterday on an afternoon when the nerves, as well as the history books, were shredded at The Hawthorns.

At just before 4.30 pm, when Albion were cruising to victory against a lacklustre Portsmouth, the Andy Johnson goal which put Crystal Palace 2–1 up at Charlton Athletic killed the carnival atmosphere at a stroke. For several minutes, rumours of a second Charlton goal swept the stadium, only to be proved false.

Then, at last, Jonathan Fortune did snatch the lifeline from Palace's grasp. After an anxious wait, with many Albion supporters turning their backs on the action to implore the press box for news from South London, the ground erupted into cacophonous celebrations.

Robson had asked the Albion fans not to come on to the pitch if they wanted their heroes to do a lap of honour. Fat chance: the playing surface was quickly a sea of striped shirts, while the West Brom battle hymn, *The Lord's My Shepherd* and the theme from *The Great Escape* echoed around the ground.

The Portsmouth followers, while disappointed to see their own side end the campaign in such supine fashion, seemed more than compensated by the news of Southampton's demise. *Harry and Jim, they're going down,* they gloated, with the Albion faithful only too happy to join in before belting out a chorus of the refrain often directed at them in the first half of the season: *Premier League, you're having a laugh.*

When the playing surface was eventually cleared, thousands of supporters massed around the touchlines, held back by rows of stewards and police. Only a phalanx of photographers and the two Albion mascots remained as the players emerged to acclaim what was possibly as disbelieving as it was delirious.

Perhaps nobody should have been unduly surprised by the last-day turnaround at the foot of the Premiership. On each of the previous two weekends, the team lying in 20th place at kick-off had ended the afternoon one rung above the drop zone. Albion knew that they had to beat Portsmouth to have any chance of repeating the feat, and even then they had to hope for the other results to go their way.

During a tense and scrappy first half, it appeared that great escape might prove to be the great anti-climax. Portsmouth, free from relegation worries several weeks ago, played the more composed football while suggesting that they might not fight too fiercely in the event of falling behind.

Albion looked understandably anxious, often misplacing passes and slicing clearances. They could easily have fallen behind after only 12 minutes, when Ricardo Fuller sent his shot wide after being put through the centre by Gary O'Neil. Robert Earnshaw had earlier missed a gilt-edged opportunity for Albion, side-footing wide after the ball was rolled in from the left by Richardson.

Yet the home side, having gone in at half-time to learn that things were going their way – and that one goal might be enough to save them – came out with a renewed sense of purpose after the break.

An injury to Jonathan Greening shortly before the hour proved a blessing in disguise for Robson. On came Horsfield, and within 20 seconds the former hod carrier from Halifax had broken the deadlock. The goal followed a cross by Zoltan Gera. The ball clipped the head of the Dejan Stefanovic before dropping obligingly to Horsfield as he lurked beyond the far post. The substitute's first touch volleyed the ball through the grasp of Jamie Ashdown, and Albion began to believe.

They made the game safe with 15 minutes remaining – and once more Horsfield was involved. A deft back-heeled pass found Richardson, the on-loan midfielder from Manchester United, who capped a display brimming with industry and invention with a calmly taken goal. There was nothing calm about the scenes that followed.

Robson, whose appointment was not universally popular with the

Albion faithful, emerged from the mayhem to admit that, 'the gods were looking down on us'. He added: 'It was a motivational thing. I've said all the way along that there's no reason why the team who are bottom at Christmas have to go down. I told the players, "Let's make history to make sure we stay in the Premiership." The lads took that on board and made sure that it happened.'

West Bromwich Albion (4-4-2): Kuszczak; Albrechtsen, Gaardsoe, Clement, Robinson; Gera, Wallwork, Richardson, Greening (Horsfield, 58 minutes); Campbell, Earnshaw (Kanu, 85 minutes). **Substitutes not used:** Murphy, Moore, Inamoto.

Portsmouth (4-4-2): Ashdown; Primus, Stefanovic, De Zeeuw, Taylor; O'Neil, Cissé, Hughes (Skopelitis, 45 minutes), Kamara (Rodic, 66 minutes); Fuller, Keene (Mezague, 81 minutes). **Substitutes not used:** Chalkias, Duffy.

Goals: Horsfield (58 minutes) 1–0; Richardson (75 minutes) 2–0.
- **Referee:** M Riley (W Yorkshire). • **Booked:** Portsmouth Fuller.
- **Man of the match:** Richardson. • **Attendance:** 27,751.

Although the defender achieved two promotions at the Baggies, the 'Great Escape' in 2004–05 is the season Robinson remembers most fondly.

'That was an amazing season and turn around. Obviously ten points adrift at Christmas, not having a hope in hell and everyone just writing us off, then we managed to turn it around. We got together as a group of players and realised what we needed to do and a lot of credit has to go to Bryan Robson for doing that as well as Nigel Pearson, who was assistant manager at the time. They made us work hard and determined and it was an unbelievable achievement. It was up and down all day really because we kept getting the vibes from the crowd. We were getting told what was happening between Charlton Athletic and Crystal Palace and you could hear the sighs of the crowd when Palace scored, even though we were doing our job by winning. When I was taking throw-ins the fans were shouting "Palace are winning 2–1 Robbo" and we couldn't do much else. When the final whistle went we didn't know Charlton had equalised and then it just went into madness.'

The following season the Baggies were typical of the club's yo-yo stereotype with two relegations and a promotion as Champions before the whole hearted defender joined Bolton on loan before making the move permanent.

I am sure The Gaffer would have preferred the champagne down his throat!

MEMORABLE GAME 9

BIRM CITY 2 – WEST BROM ALBION 0 • 29 October 2006

Bruce furious at Robinson elbow by Neil Moxley

Tony Mowbray is facing the first serious test of his managerial career at the Hawthorns as a war of words erupted over an elbowing incident involving West Bromwich Albion defender Paul Robinson.

The new Baggies chief will have to decide today how to deal with the serious accusations of Birmingham boss Steve Bruce as an almighty row kicked off between the two clubs following this feisty derby at St Andrew's.

The rumpus centred on an incident five minutes from the end of an otherwise entertaining game when Robinson clashed with Birmingham captain Damien Johnson, who was taken to hospital with a broken jaw and will see a specialist today to determine whether he needs surgery.

Bruce likened the challenge to Ben Thatcher's on Pedro Mendes in August, claiming that the defender had deliberately raised his arm to intentionally hurt the Northern Ireland international.

Referee Nigel Miller dismissed Robinson while Mowbray will study video evidence today before deciding on his course of action. He declined an offer to view the pictures immediately after the match.

In August, Manchester City boss Stuart Pearce pre-empted any Football Association action by instigating his own over Thatcher. However, television replays, while not showing Robinson in particularly good light, are inconclusive.

Bruce said: 'It was a horrific challenge on Damien. We've got to stamp that out, it was an elbow. I've seen it repeatedly on television and it's a horror show.

'Robinson knew what he was doing. That was a deliberate elbow across his face.'

But Robinson, defending himself, pointed the finger of blame straight back at the home midfielder.

He said: 'It was a 50-50 ball and I actually pulled out of the tackle because I saw Damien coming in with his foot up. I jumped out of the way to protect myself. That's the only reason my feet left the ground.

'Because of the speed at which we were both going for the ball, there was no way I could get out of the way and I have a big bruise on my ribcage from the collision. The linesman, who was close to the incident, did not even flag for a foul and I was astonished when the referee showed me a red card. There is absolutely no way I would deliberately try to hurt or "do" a fellow professional. I wish Damien all the best.'

Paul went to see Damien Johnson in the physiotherapist's room after the match, but Johnson refused to accept his apology!

Match Report:

Double goalscorer Gary McSheffrey, who returns to his former club Coventry City with Birmingham tomorrow night, paid tribute to Johnson for getting to his feet after being floored, but was prepared to give the accused the benefit of the doubt. The row overshadowed two high quality finishes from the £2.3million man – although he was pipped for the man-of-the-match award by Arsenal youngster Fabrice Muamba who was a towering figure in Birmingham's midfield.

McSheffrey said: 'I know Robbo quite well, he's an honest lad and will give his all and I just think he went over the ball a bit and caught him in the face. I don't think he would go to hurt anyone intentionally'.

'When you see the incident you will be as appalled as I am because my captain is on the way to hospital with a suspected broken jaw,' said the Birmingham manager. 'He knew what he was doing, the full-back. I've got big admiration for him as a player but that was intentional. It was absolutely disgraceful.'

Albion were trailing to Gary Mcsheffrey's superb early free-kick when Robinson clashed with Johnson. The West Bromwich full-back controlled a cross-field ball but then lost his footing and, as he sought to make up ground, clattered into the Northern Ireland international.

His arm made contact with Johnson's face, leaving the Birmingham captain prone and briefly unconscious. Albion's players remonstrated with Nigel Miller's decision to show a red card, although there was little cause for complaint.

Indeed, Mowbray's players had contributed to their own downfall all afternoon, missing numerous chances and allowing McSheffrey, who has hitherto struggled to justify the £2.3million Bruce paid for him in August, the freedom to wreak havoc and ease the pressure that has been mounting on his manager. This was Birmingham's third straight win after five matches without a victory, closing the gap on Albion to just one point.

McSheffrey's first goal arrived after a sustained period of Albion pressure, but the Baggies' failure to turn one of those chances into goals proved costly when Chris Perry got too tight to Cameron Jerome at the opposite end. McSheffrey stepped forward to curl a superb 25-yard free-kick into the top corner.

Birmingham were liberated, the goal imbuing Bruce's side with belief. In midfield Stephen Clemence and Fabrice Muamba snapped into tackles while up front Jerome and Nicklas Bendtner tracked back, making life uncomfortable for their opponents. Albion's threat had not diminished, though, and the visitors were entitled to feel aggrieved before the interval when Miller waved away appeals for a penalty after Diomansy Kamara, bursting into the Albion area, appeared to be caught by Martin Taylor.

Twice McSheffrey ought to have extended Birmingham's lead, heading straight at Pascal Zuberbuhler and then firing a close-range shot at the Albion goalkeeper's legs. Those misses were forgotten, though, when the winger sashayed around Perry before deftly chipping Zuberbuhler.

Perhaps Steve Bruce's over-the-top (no pun intended) reaction was fuelled by the fact that in an April 1983 match against Newport County he attempted, in a moment of anger, to deliberately injure opposition player Tommy Tynan, but connected awkwardly and succeeded only in breaking his own leg, leaving him unable to play again for six months.

'I fully understand people's reaction and frustration looking at me as a thug-type player, which I am not. There was no way I intentionally went out to do Damien Johnson, it was totally by accident and I was apologising to him after the game. When I have the reputation like I have in the game, everyone likes to jump on the bandwagon. Steve Bruce didn't help with his press releases; he made it pretty hellish for my family, and me so that was tough to take. This is football; certain players have to deal with this sort of stuff.'

West Bromwich Albion: Zuberbuhler, Albrectson, Davies, Perry, Robinson (Sent off), Gera (Yellow card), Greening, Quashie (Hartson 67 minutes), Koumas, Kamara (Yellow Card), Ellington.

Birmingham City: Taylor Maik, Kelly, Jaidi, Taylor Martin, Sadler, Johnson, Muamba (Danns 89 minutes), Clemence (Nafti 76 minutes), McSheffrey, Bendtner, Jerome (Larsson 67 minutes).
Scorer: McSheffery – 19 minutes, 90 minutes

Attendance: 21,009 • **Referee:** N. Miller.

The incident was reported in the national press as follows:

'On 28 October 2006, Birmingham City captain Damien Johnson's jaw was broken in two places in a collision with Paul Robinson during a local derby, for which he received a straight red card. The incident drew criticism from Birmingham manager Steve Bruce, who believed Robinson's use of the elbow was a deliberate act. The collision occurred in the dying minutes of the match, which Birmingham won 2–0 at St. Andrew's. Robinson protested his innocence immediately whilst Johnson went off to see a specialist to determine whether he required surgery or not. "For me, this one is just as bad as the Ben Thatcher (See Note below) incident a couple of weeks ago," fumed Blues boss Steve Bruce. "Robinson has turned his whole body to make sure he gets his elbow through. That can only damage people. It was horrific, it was awful and it was intended. He knew what he was doing. I don't think in my 10 years of management I've ever criticised any individual but the more I see that challenge; the more I am appalled by it. I like Robinson as a player. I think he is the best full-back in the Championship but there is no need, especially in the light of what has happened in recent weeks, to mount a challenge like that." Robinson is now facing a three-match ban for violent conduct.'

Note: The 'Ben Thatcher incident' to which Steve Bruce referred happened on 23 August 2006 when the Manchester City defender elbowed Portsmouth's Pedro Mendes in a goalless draw. He received an eight-match ban from the Football Association for violent conduct.

MEMORABLE GAME 10

DERBY COUNTY 1 – WEST BROM ALBION 0 • 28 May 2007

Match Report:

Stephen Pearson scored the only goal as Derby County defeated West Bromwich Albion to win the Championship Play-off Final and claim a place in next season's Premiership. West Bromwich Albion dominated large periods, with Stephen Bywater denying Diomansy Kamara, Jason Koumas and Paul Robinson, while Kevin Phillips hit the crossbar. Dean Kiely saved a Paul Peschisolido strike and a shot from Matt Oakley. But he could not stop Pearson converting Giles Barnes's low cross as Derby won a promotion worth £60m

The result is a triumph for Rams boss Billy Davies, who had failed in the previous two Championship play-off campaigns with former club Preston North End.

But the Scot has ended his first season at Pride Park by guiding Derby back to the top flight for the first time since 2002.

The Rams had finished the regular season eight points clear of West Bromwich Albion – but Tony Mowbray's Baggies played the bulk of the football in the Final and can consider themselves unfortunate to lose.

The match had started at a cracking pace, with Derby struggling to contain West Bromwich Albion's early surges. As early as the first minute Bywater was forced into a decent diving save to thwart Kamara. Derby's league campaign was built upon their determination, resilience and mean defence – and these qualities proved to be the foundation for their final victory.

But an early sparkling run from Koumas threatened to unlock it completely and it took a brilliant last-ditch sliding tackle from Tyrone Mears to stop the Wales international. The Rams spent most of the opening period trying to force their way into the contest - but they did have one excellent chance after 10 minutes. Howard played Peschisolido into a huge gap in the centre of the West Bromwich Albion back line but the 36-year-old, surprisingly recalled to the starting line-up, made a poor connection with his strike and Kiely saved easily.

A jinking run from Craig Fagan saw the Birmingham-born forward cut in from the right touchline and shoot narrowly wide. But after an open end-to-end start to the final, both teams gradually cancelled each other out.

Koumas looked the most likely to provide the missing inspiration and, after cutting inside with 40 minutes gone, drilled his strike narrowly over the crossbar. And Phillips ensured West Brom ended the half in the ascendancy with a crisp 20-yard strike that grazed the crossbar after a flowing move opened up the Rams defence.

West Bromwich Albion continued to create chances after the break – Bywater saving from Koumas and Kamara curling a free-kick over the bar. Derby, in contrast, struggled to impose themselves on the match and Davies introduced Barnes for Peschisolido after 59 minutes. And seconds later Derby almost scored when Oakley, who had pulled a shot wide earlier, made a brilliant contact with a Fagan cross only to be denied by Kiely's finger-tip save.

But with 61 minutes gone Derby, somewhat against the run of play, did score. Howard played in Barnes to drill a low pass across the face of goal and Pearson got inside Paul McShane and slotted home his first goal for Derby to spark scenes of jubilation.

Having made most of the running for most of the match, the Baggies continued to press, with Bywater requiring two attempts to claim a strike from Zoltan Gera. Bywater saved a Robinson header and most of the remainder of the game was played in the Derby half but West Bromwich Albion could find no way to goal.

Derby: Bywater, Mears, Leacock, Moore, McEveley, Fagan (Edworthy 83 minutes), Oakley, Seth Johnson (Jones 87 minutes), Pearson, Howard, Peschisolido (Barnes 58minutes).

Substitutes Not Used: Camp, Macken.

Booked: Peschisolido, Mears, Bywater, Oakley, Jones.

Goal: Pearson 61 minutes.

West Bromwich Albion: Kiely, McShane (Ellington 71 minutes), Perry, Sodje (Clement 81 minutes), Robinson, Koumas, Greening, Gera (Carter 71 minutes), Koren, Kamara, Phillips.

Substitutes Not Used: Daniels, Chaplow.

Booked: Sodje, McShane, Perry.

Attendance: 74,993 • **Ref:** G Poll (Hertfordshire).

MEMORABLE GAME 11

WEST BROM ALBION 0 – PORTSMOUTH 1 • 6 April 2008

A second-half goal from Kanu was enough to send Portsmouth through to its first FA Cup Final in 69 years.

Match Report:

Ex-West Bromwich Albion striker Kanu side-footed an easy chance to see off the Baggies after Dean Kiely had denied Milan Baros and Zoltan Gera had failed to clear. Baros, who looked to have handled in the build-up to the goal, missed a simple chance to seal the win. They were almost made to pay but Robert Koren's shot hit the bar and Ishmael Miller fired wide late on. Portsmouth will face the winners of the all-Championship semi-final tie between Barnsley and Cardiff on Sunday in the Final.

Their win carries on the top flight's run of having a team in every FA Cup Final. Pompey were already odds-on favourites to lift the trophy before the game, but for long periods it was West Bromwich Albion who looked the better bet for a return to Wembley on 17 May. Harry Redknapp's south coast side were not at the races during a lacklustre first-half display and it was Albion who looked like the Premier League thoroughbreds. Portsmouth's defensive pair of Sol Campbell and Sylvain Distin struggled throughout to deal with veteran forward Kevin Phillips dropping deep.

The former Southampton striker found plenty of space and tested Pompey early on with a long-range shot just over the bar before a neat lay-off that ended with Zoltan Gera causing problems for a fumbling David James with a low shot.

Portsmouth were all at sea going forward, with Baros wasteful and Kanu barely contributing as Redknapp looking increasingly agitated on the sidelines. They enjoyed their best spell of the first half shortly before the break but Redknapp, on his first appearance in the FA Cup semi-finals and at Wembley as player or manager, would have had strong words at the interval. There appeared to be little immediate change in Pompey's play, but less than 10 minutes after the break they broke the deadlock. Glen Johnson played a ball into Baros, who may have controlled the ball with his arm before getting off a shot which Kiely did well to keep out

However as Kiely looked to pounce on the loose ball Gera tried to clear and could only steer the ball into the direction of Kanu to slot into the empty net from only a couple of yards out. It should have been game over as Baros was played in by a slide rule pass from Niko Kranjcar and seemed certain to score, but he made an awful hash of the finish and Kiely produced a desperate save. The Baggies almost made them pay as the game burst into life in the latter stages. Carl Hoefkens set up Koren and his shot beat James but smacked the top of the bar. Moments later substitute Miller got clear on the left and tried to pick out Phillips at the back post, but James anticipated well and plucked his cross out of the air. There were further worries as Hoefkens sidestepped an on-rushing Miller but he side-footed wide and Pompey survived to book their place in the final.

West Bromwich Albion: Kiely, Hoefkens, Albrechtsen, Clement, Robinson, Morrison (Brunt 60 minutes), Koren, Gera (Kim 75 minutes), Greening, Bednar (Miller 60 minutes), Phillips.
Substitutes Not Used: Danek, Pele.

Portsmouth: James, Johnson, Campbell, Distin, Hreidarsson, Diarra, Diop, Muntari, Kranjcar, Kanu (Davis 80 minutes), Baros (Nugent 71 minutes).
Substitutes Not Used: Ashdown, Lauren, Pedro Mendes.

Booked: Baros. • **Goal:** Kanu 54 minutes. • **Attendance:** 83,584. • **Ref:** Howard Webb (England).

Obviously I am still in touch with Kevin Phillips (See 'Foreword') but I am also in contact with Johnathan Greening. 'Jonno' was superb for us, and he always wanted the ball even in ridiculous positions. You need those people in your team. He is a good mate of mine and was my roommate for five years. On one occasion when I went back to play at Watford, he celebrated a goal the wrong way though and I did have a little word with him after the game ... I told him he was going to get me grief from my family and friends for winding the Watford fans up!'

Player Profile
Greening began his career in 1996 with York City but moved to Manchester United in 1998, with whom he won the 1998–99 UEFA Champions League as a non-playing substitute in the Final. However, he failed to make a breakthrough in the Manchester United first team and followed United assistant manager Steve McLaren to Middlesbrough in 2001. In 2004, he joined West Bromwich Albion for £1.25 million, and in 2008, captained the team to the Championship title. Greening made his Albion debut in a 1–1 draw away at Blackburn Rovers on the opening day of the 2004–05 Premier League season, and quickly established himself as a key player in the Baggies' midfield, helping to secure their Premier League survival in his first season. He was named Albion's Player of the Year in the 2005-06 in which he made 41 appearances and scored two goals as the club was relegated to the Championship

He signed a new three-year contract with Albion in August 2007 and was made club captain for the 2007–08 season. He captained Albion in the FA Cup semi-final, where they lost 1–0 to Portsmouth and one month later led the team to promotion as winners of the Championship. Greening was named in the 2007–08 season Championship PFA Team of the Year, alongside teammates Paul and Kevin Phillips. Towards the end of the 2008–09, Greening said he was looking to sign a new contract with Albion. He was offered a new four-year contract by the club, but instead handed in a transfer request in July 2009. He signed for Fulham in 2009 he then moved on to

Nottingham Forest in 2011 staying for three years. Now on a semi-professional contract with Tadcaster Albion. He made 196 appearances for The Baggies scoring seven goals.

During my time at The Hawthorns there were three captains that impressed me Andy Johnson, Sean Gregan and Darren Moore.

Andrew James Johnson joined the Baggies for £200,000 from Nottingham Forest making 133 senior appearances during the period 2001–2006 scoring seven goals. He left to join Leicester City in June 2006.

Sean Matthew Gregan scored two goals in 79 senior appearances during his spell with the Albion from 2002–04 joining from Preston North End in August 2000 for a fee of £2million he left to join Leeds United.

Darren Mark Moore joined the Albion from Portsmouth on 14 September 2001 for a fee of £750,000. He was sent off just once in over 100 games for the Baggies in January 2006, which proved to be his last game in the blue and white stripes signing for Derby County for a fee of £300,000. He was known by the supporters as Big Dave after a character in a Pot Noodle television advertisement. I still see Darren who is currently with the West Bromwich Albion Academy set up.

The table below shows my season-by-season appearances for The Hawthorns club:

SEASON	LEAGUE	F.A. CUP	LEAGUE CUP	OTHER	TOTAL
2003–04	31(0)	1(0)	0(0)	0(0)	32(0)
2004–05	30(1)	3(0)	0(0)	0(0)	33(1)
2005–06	33(0)	1(0)	2(0)	0(0)	36(0)
2006–07	42(2)	4(0)	3(0)	3(0)	52(2)
2007–08	43(1)	4(0)	1(0)	0(0)	48(1)
2008–09	35(0)	2(1)	0(0)	0(0)	37(1)
TOTAL	214(4)	15(1)	6(0)	3(0)	238(5)

Robbo with the Division One Runners-Up shield

5.

'Bolton Wanderers – Out on Loan'

On 12 July 2009, I completed a season-long loan move to Bolton Wanderers, where I was reunited with my former West Bromwich Albion manager Gary Megson (Note: From October 2007 to December 2009 Played 98 Won 27 Drew 45 Lost 26 Win Ratio 27.55%).

I joined Bolton Wanderers on a three-year contract, the first year being on loan and the deal to become permanent in the summer of 2010 when Bolton Wanderers would pay West Bromwich Albion a fee of £1 million.

My debut was in a 1–0 defeat to Sunderland on 15 August 2009. The deal was made permanent in January 2010. I settled in at the start making 25 league appearances in the first season, and 35 in 2010–11 season, but things changed for me when Gary Megson left the club and Owen Coyle (Note From January 2010 to October 2012 Played 126 Won 42 Drew 24 Lost 60 Win Ratio 33.33%) was appointed manager in January 2010. I did not fit into Owen Coyle's plans and therefore fell out of favour in the 2011–12 Premier League season, making only 20 appearances in total for the club.

I had left West Bromwich Albion in a deal in the summer of 2009 as I was in need of some motivation after being relegated with the Baggies. I have to admit that I allowed last season's struggle against the drop to affect my form at times.

My debut for Bolton Wanderers was against Sunderland, and I can think of no one better equipped to kick-start my career in a Bolton shirt than my former Hawthorns boss, who took me to the Midlands six years ago from Watford.

It was good to be working with him again because he got me enjoying my football again. Your confidence can take a hit when you are playing in a side that aren't winning games, as I was at West Bromwich, so sometimes you need that spark. Gary gets players fired up. Sometimes you need that when you are playing, and maybe looking like you are taking it too easy. He knows how to give you that rocket to liven you up again.

Although he still gave off the occasional verbal volley, I believe Megson was a calmer character at Bolton Wanderers than the one I played under at West Bromwich Albion.

He had changed a lot now since when he moved on from West Bromwich, He was a lot more relaxed and more involved around the lads to a certain extent. It was good to see – so for me, it was good to be back playing in his side again.

My move to Lancashire was reported in the Press as follows:

Bolton still believe they can land Albion defender Paul Robinson despite the apparent impasse between the clubs. Trotters boss Gary Megson remains confident he can strike a deal with his former club for the 30-year-old Robinson, after leaving a structured bid worth up to £1.3 million at The Hawthorns. Robinson is desperate to move to the Reebok Stadium and will try to persuade the Baggies to let him move to Lancashire in the next few days. But, despite being willing to let Robinson leave, Albion officials are holding out for their valuation of the player to be met. That is believed to involve a seven figure down payment, which Megson has so far been unwilling to offer. A large portion of the current Trotters bid is tied up in add-on clauses.

The uneasy relationship between Megson and Baggies Chairman Jeremy Peace is an added complication to the transfer, which currently looks to be locked in stalemate. But Bolton officials are privately optimistic the clubs can reach an agreement on a transfer that all parties now agree would be in everyone's best interests. Meanwhile, Trotters sources have dismissed fresh stories claiming Megson will make a move for Baggies captain Jonathan Greening …

A captain that impressed me was Kevin Davies who made 407 appearances in a ten-year spell at Bolton scoring 85 goals.

Kevin Cyril Davies (born 26 March 1977) made his name as a vital part of the Chesterfield team which reached the semi-finals of the FA Cup in 1997. He left Chesterfield at the end of that season, having made 148 appearances for the club and joined Premier League side Southampton in May 1997. He only spent one season at Southampton, making 30 appearances, before he joined Premier League side Blackburn Rovers in a club-record £7.5 million deal. Once again, he spent a single season at the club, making 29 appearances, before re-joining Southampton in 1999. In his second spell at the club, he made 95 appearances, also spending part of 2002 on loan to Division One side Millwall where he made nine appearances. Released by Southampton at the end of the 2002–03 he joined Premier League side Bolton Wanderers on a free transfer. He was made Bolton team captain in January 2009, but began to fall out of favour at Bolton towards the end of the 2012–13 season and the club decided against renewing his contract. He joined current club Preston North End in July 2013.

It's been reported that I never got on with Owen Coyle, however this is not true, yes things got tough for me towards the end of my time at Bolton, but you have to dig in deep and get on with it. Coyle gave the Bolton players a glimpse of Wembley just before our FA Cup semi-final against Stoke City. Here is how the press reported the matter:

Robinson says that tactic could prove to be a masterstroke by the manager. He feels the team will now be relaxed and ready to go when they walk out to face Stoke in the FA Cup semi-final at the national stadium.

The former West Bromwich Albion and Watford full-back said after a visit to the stadium this week: 'You can see the manager's point of view in taking us to Wembley. There are a lot of young players in our team who are not used to the surroundings and what it is like. It was a great opportunity for them to go with their cameras and take their pictures as well as see a fantastic stadium and take it all in.

Robinson has fallen twice at the semi-final hurdle of the competition, first with Watford in 2003 when they lost to Southampton. Then in 2008 he was part of the West Bromwich side that were beaten by eventual winners Portsmouth.

Robinson said: 'I hope the phrase third time lucky rings true with me. The FA Cup is very special.

It is the best cup in the world and one you want to win. Unfortunately for me it has ended twice at the semi-final stage, so I will be doing my best to push us further.'

Robinson hopes the excitement of the Stoke showdown is not too much for his wife Caroline. She is due to give birth to their fourth child in five weeks at the end of May. Robinson said: 'My best hope given my wife's situation is we don't go into extra time and penalties! Luckily for me she will have family all around her, so she will be in good hands. Fingers crossed the baby won't come early.

Bolton go into the match on the back of a thumping home victory against West Ham and Robinson credits Coyle for changing the mentality of the players. Coyle arrived in January last year from Burnley and kept the club in the top flight when they were favourites to be relegated. This season they have kicked on under the Glasgow-born boss and lie eighth in the table, winning plaudits for their easy-on-the-eye style of play.

Robinson said: 'Owen Coyle has brought a togetherness back. He has made the players confident in their own ability. It has shown throughout the season because you can see how far we have come. We have all stuck together. We are in a good moment. It has been a great season so far. We have to keep going, that's the trick.

My reputation continued to haunt me at Bolton. Arsene Wenger, Arsenal's manager said I should have seen a red card for my 'horror tackle' (Wenger's words not mine!) on Abou Diaby when Arsenal hosted Bolton on 11 September 2011 and it was then I began to realise the power of social media to be disruptive and cruel. The problem with elements of social media is the anonymity it provides thereby allowing 'mystery' bloggers to issue throughout the Internet this type of personal attack.

BLOG BEGINS

*After the match Wenger and many others in the blogosphere, thought the press was curiously quiet on the issue, highlighted the fact that Robinson looked to have gone in to do Diaby. Flying in, studs up, over the ball, Robinson somehow misses the ball entirely and only connects with Diaby's standing leg. Robinson could have won the ball without hitting Diaby is possibly the most damning evidence that the tackle was more intentional than the Bolton defender would like you to believe. It seems though that while Robinson can't tackle he sure can read and what he has been reading he can parrot back when asked by a reporter. You will be shocked to find that he uses **all** of the cliches that Arsenal supporters have grown to love hearing whenever some thug tries (or succeeds) to break an Arsenal player's leg: he's not that kind of player, Wenger is moaning, it wasn't a bad tackle, the speed of the game is to blame, and people who say that's a bad tackle want to turn football into a non-contact sport. Robinson's comments are: It's typical Arsene – an Arsenal player gets hurt and he goes public like that.*

- I am not that type of player, I am fully committed, I am 100 per cent. I am not going to change that until I hang up my boots.

- I have seen it again and it was a good, hard tackle. When you slide in like that, it's impossible to get out of the way.

- Are we going to ban tackling? It's ridiculous. It's part of the sport. If we stop people tackling, it will become a non-contact game.

- I have got injured going into tackles in the past because I am committed. These things happen. There is nothing you can do about it.

- I have seen a lot worse anyway. But when it happens to an Arsenal player it is blown out of all proportion.

The one thing that he says in here that is indisputable is that Paul Robinson has seen worse, because Paul Robinson has actually done worse. His claim that 'he's not that kind of player' is laid bare when you hark back to a little incident that happened when Birmingham played Robinson's then team West Bromwich Albion

Again, that was Steve Bruce who said that he felt Paul Robinson intentionally broke Damien Johnson's jaw. That's not 'Whinging Wenger' or the latest bon mot 'The Nutty Professuer' that's good old English through and through, hard-nosed, no nonsense Steve Bruce saying that Paul Robinson is, in fact, that kind of guy.

Bruce's quote also shows how Robinson's other cliches are also just a bunch of bunk. Does Steve Bruce want to turn football into a non-contact sport? Hardly.

Is only Arsene Wenger complaining about vicious fouls? Hardly.

So on down the line. Every single cliche that the press has pushed this season and that was parroted here by Paul Robinson is false.

In the end though, I don't really blame Paul Robinson. He's just a footballer and a footballer with a horrible reputation to boot, so of course he is eager to repeat the tired warhorses that the press have been beating all season. He probably figures it will do him some good to shift the blame away from his seemingly intentional tackle on Diaby and onto the target du jour; Arsene Wenger.

Who I blame here is the press directly. Unlike a blogger, footballer, or even a football manager, they have a responsibility to provide balanced coverage. A balanced story there would have included at least some mention of Robinson's nine red cards or maybe a counter quote from Steve Bruce or another manager. But instead, they simply ask him what he thinks and let it stand.

They do this because his quotes support the narrative that they have developed and want to perpetuate. When confronted, they can now say 'it's not just us, footballers like Paul Robinson think Wenger is a whiner, that people want to make football a non-contact sport, that these players aren't bad guys, and that these aren't even hardly fouls.'

Looks like the echo chamber is in full effect and luckily for the press they have a willing tool in Paul Robinson."

BLOG ENDS

Paul was profiled in the Bolton Wanderer's programme against West Bromwich Albion on 26 December 2010 under the section entitled 'THE PLAYER' by Robert Urbani

Bolton Wanderers Programme

A man of the match performance against Blackburn Rovers two weeks ago and an ever-present in the Barclays Premier League so far this season, Paul Robinson has made the left-back position his own. The Watford-born defender has been a model of consistency since the first ball was kicked back in August, offering whole-hearted and committed performances every time he has taken the field, none more so than against the men from Ewood Park. A popular man in the dressing room too 'Robbo' typifies the fighting spirit, which has seen Wanderers move into the upper echelons of the league table over the course of the first five months of the campaign. Robinson, who tackles his former club this afternoon, spoke to the official match day programme ahead of today's showdown to offer his assessment of how the 2010–11 season is progressing and what Wanderers can expect from the Baggies – the club he made over 230 appearances for between 2003 and 2009.

Paul, a man of the match performance against Blackburn in our last home game, how much did you enjoy that result?
As you could probably tell, I thoroughly enjoyed it and I thought we were worthy winners. We knew what the game would be like against Blackburn – very physical with plenty of long balls. I thought that we dealt with their periods of attacking pressure very well and every player was first-class. I've got to give credit to every single one of the players, who have been giving 100 percent, week in week out. There will be times when we aren't going to get the right results but no one can fault the effort. So it was nice to have won the award and I'm pleased with the way I'm playing, but it's a collective team effort.

We are approaching the midway point of the season. What's your verdict on how the first five months have transpired?
It's been a very good start. It's probably been much better than everybody expected but, as a group of players, we all thought that we could do well, make progress from last season and push up the league table

and give the fans a team to be proud of. However, we've got to remember that we have only played 18 Premier League games, and there is a lot of football still left to be played this season. We have to keep going and make sure that we don't find ourselves in a position where we are looking over our shoulders.

The festive period is a time of year when a lot of people are off work and enjoying time at home with their families. For a footballer it is very different with so many matches in a short space of time. How do you find this time of the year?

Christmas is a difficult time of the year in terms of travelling and being away from your family. You don't get to enjoy the festivities like a lot of other people but we get breaks in other parts of the year. A lot of people enjoy letting their hair down on Christmas Day and eating plenty of food, but we're in training, preparing, because there's always the Boxing Day fixture. It's important to remain very professional and do everything possible to make sure that you are fully focused on the game. It is tough making the sacrifices but you always need to remind yourself that we, as footballers, are doing a privileged job that we all love and playing football over Christmas is part and parcel. We can't complain and I'm happy for it to be this way until the time comes when I have to hang up my boots.

On the field, it's also an important time of the year. There are so many games in quick succession that it can have a big influence on the shape of the season?

Obviously there is today's game and Wigan to come shortly too and people might see them as 'winnable' games. But we treat every match the same because there are no easy matches in the Premier League. It's important that we are not complacent, are positive and look to get on the front foot as early as possible in all of those matches.

You obviously get to play against your former club today. How do you summarise your time at The Hawthorns?

We played West Brom in October and that was a special day for me. There was a mixture of emotions but I felt that perhaps a 1–1 draw was the right result on the day, given the way that the two teams played. It was nice to see plenty of familiar faces and it was also especially pleasing to get a round of applause from the real fans that supported me throughout the six years that I had there. I was the last player off the pitch because I wanted to show my appreciation. I clapped the Bolton fans first because I obviously play for their club now, and then the West Brom supporters because I didn't get a chance to say my farewells before I left.

From your point of view, are you pleased to see West Brom making the most of another opportunity to play in the Premier League?

Of course I am. They have had some great results this season, especially winning at Arsenal and Everton. I know that they are associated with being a yo-yo club but Robbie (Di Matteo) is doing a fantastic job there. Hopefully we will get the chance to play against them again next year because I do believe that they will manage to stay in the league.

What was your outstanding achievement at the Hawthorns?

It was special to reach the FA Cup semi-final in 2008 and playing at Wembley was a great memory, but the year that we stayed in the Premier League in the 2004–05 season when Bryan Robson was the manager was an unbelievable achievement. Everyone thought we were dead and buried at Christmas because we only had ten points but we somehow managed to turn things around and survive. We managed to generate a fantastic team spirit and I will never forget the feeling on the last day of the season when we beat Portsmouth at home. We were bottom of the table after 37 games but results went in our favour and we stayed up. Winning promotion under Tony Mowbray in 2007–08

was also amazing. We won the Championship in style that season. I
went through the hard times and the good times at West Bromwich,
but there was a group of lads who all stuck together and I felt that the
club really did move forward in the time that I was there.

Are you still in contact with any of the players there?

Players move around, but I still speak to James Morrison, Chris Brunt,
Scott Carson, Graeme Dorrans and Jonas Olsson – they are a great
bunch of lads. It was a difficult time for them when they were in the
Premier League last time around but now they have more experience
and have a better understanding of what is needed in this league. I'm
also still close with Kevin Phillips and Jonathan Greening, who now
obviously play for Birmingham and Fulham. I speak to them quite reg-
ularly to see how they are getting on and they are both Godfathers to
my children.

It was nice to see plenty of
familiar faces and it was also
especially pleasing to get a round
of applause from the real fans
that supported me throughout
the six years that I had there. I
was the last player off the pitch
because I wanted to show my
appreciation.

Bolton Away Kit

MEMORABLE GAME 12

BOLTON WANDERERS 0 – STOKE CITY 5 • 17 April 2011

Three first-half goals helped Stoke City demolish Bolton Wanderers and reach the FA Cup Final for the first time in it's history.

Aided by some woeful Bolton defending, Matthew Etherington, Robert Huth and Kenwyne Jones scored in the first half-hour and two goals by Jon Walters after the break completed the victory. Stoke, roared on by their vociferous fans, can look forward to returning to Wembley to face Manchester City in the Final on 14 May.

Their other reward is a possible place in the Europa League, either through winning the FA Cup or if City secure fourth place in the league and enter the Champions League – which will mean the Cup runners-up gain the European spot

For Wanderers, however, the occasion was a massive anti-climax as their hopes of reaching a first final since 1958 in tribute to the late Nat Lofthouse were quickly left in ruins. Bolton were given an ominous warning in the opening minutes when they were caught napping by a quickly taken Stoke free-kick that enabled Walters to escape down the left before being denied by Jussi Jaaskelainen.

Bolton did manage a couple of efforts at the other end, with Gary Cahill blasting over from a corner and Johan Elmander failing to test Thomas Sorensen with a low shot from distance. But their big day began to disintegrate from the moment a misplaced pass by Paul Robinson found Etherington on the edge of the area and the winger composed himself before lashing a fierce shot into the corner of the net.

Things quickly got worse for Bolton and, again, their defending was at fault. Cahill got no distance on his header as he tried to clear a cross and Huth met the bouncing ball with a first-time shot that flew past Jaaskelainen's despairing dive.

In the absence of the cup-tied striker Daniel Sturridge, Bolton's only game-plan appeared to be lumping the ball towards Kevin Davies' head, a tactic that failed to create any openings. On the half-hour mark Stoke compounded their misery with a third goal. Jermaine Pennant stole the ball from Martin Petrov and made for goal, before slipping a pass through to Jones that Cahill failed to intercept, leaving the Stoke striker with an easy task to slot home.

With Bolton so poor going forward and generous in defence, the game already seemed up and to the evident frustration of their manager Owen Coyle, a comeback never looked on the cards. His response to a dismal first 45 minutes was a double change at half-time, replacing the anonymous Ivan Klasnic and the ineffective Martin Petrov with Matt Taylor and Mark Davies. Mark Davies in particular tried to get his side going but clear-cut chances for Wanderers remained elusive, while Stoke continued to threaten with their enterprising attacking play. Notably, none of the Potters' goals came from their trademark set-pieces.

Jaaskelainen kept out a Jones header and needed Robinson to block a thunderous shot from the Trinidadian. After making a hash of Etherington's chipped cross, the Bolton keeper also stopped an angled Walters effort when his defence again went missing but the Stoke forward was not to be denied a goal, making it 4–0 on 68 minutes with a rasping low shot after a fine solo run.

Stoke were not quite finished yet, with Walters getting on the end of a deflected Jones cross nine minutes from the end to notch his second of the game and put the seal on an impressive display.

Scorers: Etherington (11 minutes), Huth (17 minutes), Jones (30 minutes), Walters (68 and 81 minutes).

Bolton: Jaaskelainen (22), Steinsson (02), Robinson (4), Cahill (5), Knight (12), Muamba (6) (Moreno 73 minutes), Petrov (10), (Mark Davies 46 minutes), Lee (27), Elmander (9), Davies (12), Klasnic (17) (Taylor 46 minutes).

Substitutes: Bogdan (1), Alonso (25), Wheater (31), Taylor (7), M. Davies (16), Cohen (21) ,Moreno (19).

Stoke: Sorensen (29), Huth (4), Shawcross (17), Wilkinson (28), Whelan (6), Wilson (12), Pennant (16), (Whitehead 78 minutes), Delap (24), Etherington (26) (Pugh 87 minutes), Jones (9) (Fuller 84 minutes), Walters (19).
Substitutes: Nash (27), Faye (25), Pugh (14), Diao (15), Whitehead (18), Fuller (10), Carew (22).

Booked: Bolton: Robinson, Cahill. • **Referee:** Howard Webb.
  • **Attendance:** 75,064.

The following article appeared in the Lancashire press, which gave Paul the opportunity to express his opinion on some of the issues that have been part of his career to date.

Choosing a career highlight can often be a difficult task. Take Paul Robinson, Bolton Wanderers' durable full-back, for example.

Robinson could easily cite any of the three promotions to the Premier League with two different teams, including one as a 21-year-old with his hometown club.

Or he could select staying up in the most dramatic of fashions with West Bromwich Albion on the final day of the 2004–05 Premier League season. The three England Under-21 caps he won will also feature predominately in his pantheon of achievements.

The nadir? Well, there is no ambiguity there.

It came in December 2004, three days before his 26th birthday. Robinson found himself in the wilderness for a 10-game spell after Bryan Robson, the Manchester United legend, had replaced Gary Megson as the manager of West Bromwich Albion.

He was not even in the squad, yet attended the game with Charlton Athletic on 11 December, 2004 with his son, Luke, and wife, Caroline, to give his teammates some moral support.

Hopes of being recalled after the 1–0 defeat were no doubt discussed with his wife as he pulled on to the drive of his newly built home in Stratford-upon-Avon, the picturesque town in middle England where William Shakespeare was born. What happened next would not have looked out of place in one of the playwright's tragedies. Robinson takes up the story.

'We all went to the game and when we came back the whole house had been ransacked – everything had been taken,' he said. 'They took all the jewellery, ripped the safe out the floor, stole the TVs, DVD players and drove my wife's car off the drive. It was devastating for us and the low point in our lives.'

Of some consolation was that the burglars did not take the Christmas presents.

Robinson, 32, also looks back with regret at how he handled a situation that saw him and Watford, his hometown club, pay a substantial six-figure sum in an out-of-court settlement after a tackle by the defender fractured Stuart Talbot's shin bone in 1999.

'I just caught the top of the ball and when you go in for a tackle at speed you physically can't stop yourself,' Robinson said.

'It was a horrible time. It was tough for me to handle that I had done that to a fellow professional.

'I had no intention of going out to hurt him and did not know how bad it was at the time. When I went down the tunnel and the players and the manger were shouting abuse at me, I realised it was bad.

'I wish I had kept in touch and seen how he was doing but I had left it too long,' Robinson said. 'I regret that. I should have apologised and got my side across sooner. I was still young at the time and had no support. No one said to phone him or send him flowers and wish him a speedy recovery.'

Instead Robinson received hate mail and endured a tough period of self-appraisal.

'It did affect me for a while,' Robinson said. 'It was in the back of my mind every time I went in for a tackle and I'd wonder whether I'd injure someone badly again or even myself.'

The incident with Talbot was not the only time he courted controversy. In 2006, a challenge with Damien Johnson left the Birmingham City winger with a broken jaw and Robinson with a three-match suspension after being sent off.

Steve Bruce, the then Birmingham manager who is now in charge of Hull City, called the challenge 'horrific' but Robinson mounts a strong defence.

'I went up for a header, turned my body and somehow his jaw has caught my elbow,' Robinson said. 'I never thought of going in with my elbow; that was never my intention.

'It was just one of those things. I learnt my lessons from before and went in to see if he was all right at full-time, and found out that he had broken his jaw and would be out for a period of time, which was devastating.'

More recently, Robinson left Abou Diaby, the leggy Arsenal midfielder, nursing an ankle injury following a robust challenge at the Emirates Stadium in October.

'We were both going for the ball,' Robinson said. 'I spoke to Jack Wilshere [the Arsenal midfielder who had been on loan at Bolton the previous season] after the game and asked if Diaby was all right.

'He said he was fine and that he has just got bruising on his ankle. Then, four days later, [Arsene] Wenger came out in the press making a big fuss about it, saying I had done it deliberately. Why did he leave it four days to come out and say that? He was just jumping on the bandwagon as the social media were making a big deal of it.'

The incidents have earned Robinson a reputation as a hard man. Even Jonathan Greening, a former teammate at West Bromwich Albion and godfather to one of his four sons, nicknamed him 'Mad Dog'.

'I've got a bad reputation,' Robinson said. 'I have NEVER looked to hurt a player when I tackle. You see tackles now and again where players don't even go for the ball.

'I am totally the opposite of that but ex-players in the media just try to stereotype me. In their day, they were going round kicking lumps out of people. If they played this game now they'd be sent off in every game.

'It's a fast and furious game now and there are times you do go for the ball and you can't stop yourself when you go sliding in. I am just the sort of player who is never going to pull out of a tackle if the ball is there to be won.'

Robinson would consider himself robust rather than reckless a word, which is bandied around too much in the media and inevitably misused (Note: The Oxford English Dictionary definition of reckless is 'without thought or care for the results of an action'). He's more committed than careless but his abrasive manner on the field is in stark contrast to his affable nature off it. He is a devoted husband and father to his four sons and has a compassionate side.

A teammate of Fabrice Muamba confirmed all the Bolton Wanderers players underwent routine tests on their heart in the summer and said more regular checks should be administered during the season. Muamba is fighting for his life in a London hospital after he collapsed during a match against Tottenham Hotspur following a heart attack. Medical staff took two hours to get his heart beating normally again and the 23-year-old remains under sedation.

Paul Robinson, the Bolton left-back who joined Leeds United on loan last month, said he was 'devastated' and 'totally shocked' when he learnt the news and described the former Arsenal and Birmingham City midfielder as 'one of the fittest lads I know'.

'We all had a heart scan at the start of the season,' Robinson told *The National*. 'I don't really understand how it works but they [the medical team] put a monitor to your heart and check the beat of your heart and then get a reading. Everything was fine with me and no one else reported a problem. Fab is always up there with the best runners and is as fit as a fiddle.'

Muamba became the second Premier League player to suffer a heart problem in three months. Blackburn Rovers' Gael Givet underwent surgery in December after suffering heart palpitations during a match. Robinson called for more regular cardiac examinations.

'Perhaps it's now something we need to look at in football and do more regular testing,' Robinson, 33, said. 'You put your body through so much as a footballer and perhaps it's time for regular checks.'

Robinson had just finished playing for Leeds against West Ham United on Saturday night when news filtered through of the events unfolding at White Hart Lane.

'One of the lads [Tom Lees] got a text to say one of the players had collapsed,' Robinson said. 'My phone was on silent but when I checked it there were loads of messages. So I called my wife [Caroline] to find out who it was and she flicked on the TV and saw it was Fab. I was just devastated and I know Steve Bruce [who signed Muamba for Birmingham] was too as his son [Alex] plays with me at Leeds.'

'Fab is such a healthy lad,' Robinson said. 'He's a great athlete and a great bloke. Even though he is younger than me he is always good for advice. He's got a smile that lights up a room and is so decent and polite. He's also a top player who was an honour to play with. You knew what you got with him and he was always in people's faces on the field.'

Robinson has spoken with Owen Coyle, the Bolton manager who accompanied Muamba in the ambulance to hospital, and asked Coyle, a devout Catholic, to 'say a prayer for me'.

'The gaffer just seems in total shock as he was by his bedside and was in the ambulance with him. Just fingers crossed he is going to be OK and he pulls through.'

Fabrice and I trying to stop Manchester City's Sergio Aguero

Reflecting on his move to Bolton Wanderers Paul was reported as follows:

'The move was difficult to start with as I'd moved up on my own and my family stayed in the Midlands, which made things very testing.' The test became greater when there was a lack of first team opportunities for Robinson; this made the homesickness worse as there was no real way to get away from the frustrations the on field problems created.

While out looking for first team football on a month's loan with Leeds United, teammate and good friend Fabrice Muamba collapsed during Bolton's FA Cup quarter-final match with Tottenham Hotspur in a story that took the sporting world by storm. 'We'd literally just finished playing against West Ham United and then we had a presentation evening with the fans afterwards. We were all in this room and there were no televisions with the game on. One of the lads said, "Robbo, one of the Bolton players has collapsed on the pitch," so I got them to find out who it was, then I heard it was Fabrice. Neil Warnock pulled me to the side and told me to go home and just be with my family. I was desperate to get down to London, but there was so many people wanting to see him. I'm amazed at how much of an inspirational bloke he is with what's happened and the things he does now to promote everything. He's a shining light, an amazing person to be around and an intelligent lad, but sadly he never got the credit he deserved on the pitch.'

It was a difficult time for the Trotters and the club went downhill from there. Less than 18 months later they were relegated to the Championship and had been beaten 5–0 by Stoke at Wembley in the FA Cup semi-final.

'The lack of team spirit around the dressing room with a lot of individual players evolved around the relegation. It was a sad time for the club because it had been up there in the Premiership for ten years and it had got that stability, but now they seemed to be struggling. It was a very embarrassing performance against Stoke in the semi-final and you just wanted the ground to swallow you up. The whole place was devastated, but the worst thing about it was that we had to get ourselves up for the upcoming league games. The FA Cup is a competition the world watches so it can be a horrible place to play football sometimes.'

With Bolton's relegation fight and Robinson's contract not being renewed, the end of his time at Bolton was difficult. 'I wasn't as involved as I wanted to be, I had a lot of experience dealing with these sorts of pressures within previous seasons, but for reasons only Owen Coyle knows, I didn't get the opportunity to use them.

I am still in touch with Mark Davies, Kevin Davies and Stuart Holden.

Mark Davies – joined Bolton Wanderers in 2009 from Wolverhampton Wanderers after a loan spell with Leicester City, Still at the club with so far 136 appearances and 13 goals

Kevin Davies – joined Bolton Wanderers in 2003 from Southampton after a loan spell with Millwall. Joined Preston North End in 2013 after making 351 appearances and scoring 74 goals

Stuart Holden – joined Bolton Wanderers in 2010 from Houston Dynamo, made 30 appearances and scored two goals before going out on loan at Sheffield Wednesday in 2013.

Owen Coyle described Paul as a 'thoroughly model professional who naturally has been frustrated at not playing. This move (on loan to Leeds

United) keeps him match sharp and Leeds will benefit from his considerable top-flight experience.'

On 6 March 2012, Paul joined Leeds United on a month's loan. He was an unused substitute for their away game at Hull City the same day, and made his debut in their 2–0 win at Middlesbrough on 11 March 2012. Leeds Boss Neil Warnock described Paul, 'Paul is a player I have had my eye on for a couple of weeks. This gives us a chance to have a look at him with a view to next season'.

His loan was extended to the end of the season. He was omitted from the last game of Leeds' season, because manager Neil Warnock was unwilling to risk his suffering injury in a 'nothing' game as they were unlikely to sign him permanently. He made ten appearances for the club.

In the match day programme for Leeds United versus West Ham United on 17 March 2012 there was an article entitled 'Robbo believes in the push'.

Our new loan recruit Paul Robinson firmly believes his new teammates are more than capable of securing a Play-off spot. Paul arrived from Bolton Wanderers on the morning of our game against Hull and, even before he made his debut last weekend at Middlesbrough, he was convinced he saw enough at the KC Stadium to suggest we have every chance. 'The squad is capable of it' said Paul. 'When you make that late run you're always the favourites because you're the ones going forward. I believe in this group of players, that's why I came here. They have great ability and they're a great bunch of lads. It was a solid performance at Hull. It's a tough place to go and the pitch was bobbly. You have to grind out results at places like that and great credit to them for the way they dug in.' The trip to the KC was a swift introduction to life at Leeds for Paul after the player completed his loan move from Bolton earlier in the day. The 33-year-old joined on an initial deal until 9 April after a frustrating New Year for the player. 'I want to play some games, which I haven't been doing, and to come to a club like Leeds is a no-brainer,' said Paul, who was a near ever-present in the Bolton side before Christmas. 'It's been very frustrating for me. I feel like I was playing my best football and putting my body on the line for the club, but they obviously felt differently. I'm just happy to be away from there for a bit and hopefully play some games here. I want to get my head right here, help the lads and encourage the lads, and hopefully get to the Play-offs. I'm fit and raring to go, but I know I've got to be patient. In football you have to wait for your chance and when that comes you want to take it, and hopefully that's what'll do.' Paul says the appointment of Neil Warnock as manager was a big draw for him when Leeds came knocking. 'He's a great character in football and there's not many in the game now,' he added. 'Once I knew, I just wanted to get down here, to work with the man, and make a fresh start.'

Leeds United Action Shot

He returned to Bolton and was available for their last few matches, but was released when his contract expired at the end of the season, along with 11 other players, following the club's relegation from the Premier League.

Without a contract I had to keep myself fit until my agent Rob Segal of RS Representation got me the best deal there was for me in the game so I trained with a number of local clubs:

- Nottingham Forest – Through my friend Jonathan Greening being at the City Ground I was invited down for a trial at the request of the then manager Steve Cotterill. However on my first day he was sacked, it was not my fault I hasten to add, but it was due to new owners coming into the club on 12 July 2012. They were the Kuwati-based AL-HASAWI family. Anyway I kept my head and spent three weeks toiling away to be told by Sean O'Driscoll a deal would not be forthcoming. A few weeks later the telephone rang and it was Lee Clark and as they say the rest is history.

- Coventry City – Lee 'Carso' Carsley was the caretaker-manager at the time having been appointed on 14 February 2013

Whilst I was at Elland Road I got on well with a Brummie with whom I am still in contact:

Thomas James 'Tom' Lees – signed professional terms with Leeds United in early 2009 at the age of 18 he currently plays as a defender for Sheffield Wednesday, where he is primarily a centre-back but he can also play at right-back. He signed for The Owls at the start of 2014–15 season, after a spell at Bury before returning to Leeds United in the Summer of 2012.

Whilst I was at Leeds United I was impressed with the captaincy mentality of Robert Snodgrass and Michael Brown:

Robert Snodgrass started his senior career with Livingston. He also had a loan spell at Stirling Albion before moving to England in 2008, joining Leeds United. He helped Leeds win promotion to the Championship in 2010. In February 2012, Snodgrass was appointed captain of Leeds, but he rejected a new contract offer and moved to Norwich City in July of the same year.

Michael Robert Brown began his career with Manchester City having come through their youth scheme. He also spent time on loan at Hartlepool United, Portsmouth and Sheffield United before he was sold to Sheffield United for a £400,000 fee in January 2000.He moved to Tottenham Hotspur in January 2004 before moving on to Fulham after two years. In July 2007 he was transferred to Wigan Athletic, where he would spend two seasons before making the move to Portsmouth in August 2009. He joined Leeds United in July 2011, and went on to spend the next three years in Yorkshire before signing for Port Vale in July 2014, and also took on a coaching role with the 'Valiants'.

After I was given a free transfer at the end of the season from Bolton Wanderers I was asked if I was interested in moving to Canada as I had emerged as a target for Paul Mariner, the ex-Ipswich Town and England striker. Paul was coach of the Major League Soccer (MLS) club Toronto FC. It was a bit of a coincidence because he had already signed ex-Celtic defender Darren O'Dea who was on loan with me at Leeds United. Unfortunately it was not the right move for the family or me and the opportunity passed me by.

Club Profile

Toronto FC (TFC) is a Canadian professional soccer club based in Toronto, Ontario, which competes in Major League Soccer (MLS). Toronto became MLS's fourteenth team in the league, and first Canadian team, upon the league's expansion in 2007. The team plays home matches at the soccer-specific BMO Field, located in Exhibition Place along the Toronto lakeshore. The team is coached by Greg Vanney and operated by Maple Leaf Sports & Entertainment, which also operates the NHL's Toronto Maple Leafs, the AHL'sToronto Marlies, and the NBA's Toronto Raptors.

The clubs most significant achievement to date is winning four consecutive Canadian Championships from 2009 to 2012, and reaching the semi-finals of 2011–12 CONCACAF Champions League.

The table below shows my season-by-season appearances for the Reebok Stadium club:

SEASON	LEAGUE	FA CUP	LEAGUE CUP	OTHER	TOTAL
2009–10 (Loan)	25(0)	2(0)	0(0)	0(0)	27(0)
2010–11	35(0)	5(0)	0(0)	0(0)	40(0)
2011–12	17(0)	2(0)	1(0)	0(0)	20(0)
TOTAL	77(0)	9(0)	1(0)	0(0)	87(0)

6.

'Birmingham City'

Is it rain or sweat?

After training with the Championship club Birmingham City, I signed a one-month contract in September 2012 as a free agent after training with Nottingham Forest and Coventry City just to keep my fitness levels as high as possible. Injuries had left The Blues with only two fit senior defenders. I made my debut in the starting eleven in a 1–0 away win against Brighton & Hove Albion on 29 September 2012. After four appearances, and with the team still weakened in defence by injury, I was given a second month's contract and then a further two months after left-back David Murphy suffered knee damage. When that deal expired, and despite the club's financial difficulties, my contract was extended until the end of the season. I finished the season playing at centre-half alongside Curtis Davies, having stood in for the injured Steven Caldwell and retained my place after Caldwell's return to fitness, and made 37 appearances in all competitions in 2012–13 season.

After my first three games Lee Clark (Note: From June 2012 to October 2014 Played 116 Won 33 Drew 35 Lost 48 Win Ratio 28.4%) saluted the impact I had made since my arrival at St Andrew's. Lee Clark said: 'My signing of the former West Bromwich Albion full-back was not without controversy. Robinson's infamous clash with Damien Johnson when he was with the Baggies was not forgotten when he began training with Blues. He has made an excellent contribution from the start.'

I recall that I made what might have been a potentially tricky St Andrew's debut for Blues on 6 October 2012 against Huddersfield Town (Note: Blues 0 Huddersfield 1) but after an early full-bloodied tackle on James Vaughan (on-loan from Norwich City), the Tilton Road End and the Kop were satisfied and I went on to play shrewdly, sensibly and well. Since that moment the reception I get from the Bluenoses has been one of affection – and it's mutual.'

Lee Clark continued: 'He has been brilliant each game and when you consider the lack of matches he's had as well, and football training, it's quite remarkable. He has just showed his experience, his determination and his desire. Even when I had to put him at centre-half and brought young Mitch Hancox on in the Huddersfield Town game, he was quality then.

'His use of the ball is very good, his talking and encouragement of others is excellent. And that determination I mentioned has always been there for everyone to see. I have said it all along that the fans would take to him and I'm sure they have.'

I signed a one-year contract, with an option for a further year, ahead of the 2013–14 season, and was appointed both club and team captain for the 2013–14 season.

I was appointed captain at a particularly difficult time with so many 'ins and outs' at the start of the season, as it is the captain's responsibility to make all the newcomers feel welcome and make sure they understand the ethos of the club and the manager. At the time of my appointment we had new signings in the shape of Olly Lee from Barnet, Andrew Shinnie from Inverness Caledonian, Darren Randolph from Motherwell, Lee Novak from Huddersfield Town and Neal Eardley from Blackpool.

New contracts needed to be sorted out for Chris Burke, Akwasi Asante, Amari'i Bell and Will Packwood. There were a number of players who were contracted for the 2013–14 season but had expiry dates during the season, which can have an unsettling effect on players; Nikola Zigic (expires June 2014), David Murphy (expires June 2014), Peter Lovenkrands (expires June 2014), Marlon King (expires June 2014), Darren Ambrose (expires June 2014) and Hayden Mullins (expires June 2014). New contracts had been offered to Wade Elliott, Jonathan Spector and Colin Doyle and were awaiting decisions from the players.

Stephen Carr the previous captain had retired through serious injury and Steven Caldwell, Pablo Ibanez, Morgaro Gomis and Keith Fahey had been let go and loan deals for Jack Butland (Stoke City), Ravel Morrison (West Ham United), Paul Caddis (Swindon Town) and Shane Ferguson (Newcastle United) had expired.

Paul recalls "It was a consequence of Birmingham City's financial woes that I did not know whether I was about to go from first choice left-back to left behind. It is funny how things happen in life and in football when fate takes a hand, which on this occasion was good for me but bad luck for David Murphy who suffered a season-ending knee injury which ultimately resulted in Murphy's early retirement from the game. Once Murphy's future had been decided I knew Lee Clark would have liked to sign me for the remainder of the campaign. In November 2012 the best the club could offer was a two-month extension to my contract, after two separate one-month agreements, in November 2012. My deal was until 27 January. After that, I did not know what would happen. I honestly could not tell what was going on and I don't think anyone else knew, either. Of course it made things difficult. I had a family to look after and was trying to get my head right, it was the football that was good for me. The football takes away the thinking about it. The love of the game and playing football and enjoying it.

But it was out of my hands, there was nothing I could do about it, it was between the club and my representation. It was down to them where

I went. I had to leave the ball in their court and see what they wanted to do. But I wanted to stay; I was loving it at the Blues. The lads were brilliant, they were a great bunch and I wanted to help the club go up the league and push on. If I had had to leave, it would have been tough because of the friends I had made here and the way I was enjoying football again. The fans were brilliant, I knew before there was going to be a bit of an issue with the Jonno incident, but they knew what type of person I am. When I go out there I put my heart on my sleeve and I wear the shirt with pride. That's what I have been like at every club I have been at. I was no different at the Blues. So I was hoping that everything would get sorted to the end of the season so I could concentrate on my football more then and try and help the team get good results and push on up the league.

I could see the club's points of view on not wanting to go with a wage system that hindered them and I knew they preferred younger players and would want to bring them through, but at the time it did not help, it did not work. That was the problem. You can't do it. You have got to have experienced lads, even if experienced lads are not playing, it's always nice to have them around to encourage the others and give them confidence, to help them through tough times. Yes, I was disappointed in the summer at Bolton because you get to a certain age and you do get pushed on to this 'over-30s scrapheap'. But if you take care of yourself and you prepare yourself right, I don't see a problem.

I look at my close friend, Kev Phillips. He gives me inspiration because of what he does and how he does things. Young lads should look up to him as well – I look up to him. And I speak to him all the time for advice. I was asking him if it was me in that summer, why I wasn't being taken, and he talked to me a lot, telling me to keep going and keep working hard.

That's what I am like anyway. But it is hard training by yourself. It's that motivational thing, being around people to push you through when it's tough. I learned from it and I felt great from doing it. I never let anything affect me and I pushed myself to the limits I probably wouldn't have done before.

I am not the sprightly soul of season's yore, with the zip of a teenage full-back. But I have always done my best for the Blues so far, drawing on my experience and maintaining the abrasive edge for which I am known. And I have produced at left-back, right-back and centre-half. Eventually I would like to move into management or coaching. But at the time, another St Andrew's deal was my objective.

I was one of 19 Blues players out of contract at that time. I honestly did not know what was going to happen, but obviously I got to a position where I had to know what was going on.

If I was not going to be around the following year then I had got to plan to try and get something else. I wanted to think the club would tell me, just on a professional level and for me as well, just what I might have to try and sort out. I would absolutely love to stay, without a doubt.

I was not coming to the end of my career yet – I look at Kev, he's almost 40 – I was looking to play as long as I can. I feel good. I would love to keep working, helping the young lads here and being around. I was doing my coaching then as well, so that would help me for what I wanted to do in the future. I will be doing my UEFA B licence. When I'm finished I want to become a coach or manager, if I can.

5 June 2013 – Positive Signs

Robbo's consistent form over the final two months of the campaign was enough to persuade Blues boss Lee Clark that he could release another experienced defender, former skipper Steven Caldwell at the end of the season even though captain Stephen Carr is retiring.

Allied to his dressing room presence, he played a big part in Blues climbing away from the wrong end of the Championship to even briefly flirt as outside Play-off contenders before an ultimately respectable top-half finish.

And the work he has done in helping young Mitch Hancox along has hinted at a role on the touchline when his playing days finally come to an end.

'I'm doing my badges at the moment,' said Robinson. 'When the time is right, I'll be looking for a club to take me on the coaching side.'

With Lee Clark needing to fill the captaincy vacancy he believes that Paul Robinson is the ideal man to take on the role of Blues skipper. The 34-year-old defender has been named as both club captain and team captain by the Blues boss following the summer departures of Stephen Carr and Steven Caldwell.

'I've confirmed to Paul that he will be team and club captain next season,' said Clark. "He knows as well as I do that that doesn't guarantee him a starting position. But I think he ticks all the boxes in terms of what I'm looking for in a leader both on and off the field. He knows when the time is to give someone an arm round the shoulder and some encouragement and when the time is to give someone a kick up the backside. He also leads by example as well in terms of his performances

"I remember when we first signed him there could have been a bit of an issue but the supporters took to him very quickly and they realised whatever club he's pulling the jersey on for he gives his maximum.'

'WHO'S THE CAPTAIN?'

On 6 June 2013 website blogger Black Country Blues held an on-line discussion to debate the question.

Lee Clark has confirmed that he is still deciding who to name as the Birmingham City FC captain next season. After the retirement of skipper Stephen Carr, along with vice-captain Steven Caldwell being released, the position is open for a new leader.

Curtis Davies, who would be everyone's natural choice, is expected to be sold this summer to balance the books. Other potential candidates are David Murphy, who is expected to be fit in time for pre-season and is Blues' second longest serving player after Colin Doyle, and experienced heads such as Wade Elliott and Paul Robinson, despite the former not yet agreeing his new deal.

Nikola Zigic has been mentioned in some quarters, but his sometimes erratic nature could be disadvantageous. The giant Serb is prone to picking up a silly booking or a sending off after losing his cool. A captain has to keep their head in all situations and lead by example and it's fair to say that Zigic, at times, does not.

So, who would be your captain?

As you've said Davies would be the obvious selection but he'll be offski. I'd go for Robinson, he's an experienced old warhorse!!. (Blue Penguin 1976.)

Paul Robinson for Captain, Nicola Zigic for vice-captain (LEN.)

Robinson (L.NIVEN.)

It seems Robbo is a popular choice. Personally I'd go for a fully fit Murphy, he has been at the club for a fair while and he is arguably the best left-back in the division. Only problem being he is injury prone. (Black Horse Blue.)

Robbo for captain 100% with Curtis vice-captain (that's if he doesn't leave) (Ryan BCFC Kimbo.)

I would go for Paul Robinson; he proved himself throughout the season and has the experience. (TIRED & WEARY.)

In an ideal world you would say Paul Robinson but he will not be a full-back next season and the chances of him nailing down a central defensive position if we sign a couple of central defenders could be in doubt! David Murphy if fully fit could be a safer choice! But I do agree Robinson's attitude on and off the pitch is first class! (MATT.)

Lay off Zigic for a change! The man's a Cup Final legend! And the last man standing! (MATT.)

Maybe so, but he (Zigic) isn't captain material. See the Bolton game when he needlessly got sent off, not saying every player hasn't got that in them, but not a captain. (Black Country Blue.)

Outcome

The vastly experienced 34-year-old told BBC WM 'You're always looking over your shoulder when the end of the season comes. But I've really enjoyed my football this season and I want to stay in the game as long as I can so to get a new 12-month contract with the option of another year albeit in the club's favour is an incredible relief for me and my family.

'It was tough when I first came as I'd not played since April, but I settled in straightaway.

'The lads called me Polyfilla after all the positions I've had to fill in this season,' he joked. 'God knows what position I'm going to play in next season.'

He ended up making 37 appearances, latterly as a makeshift centre-half, alongside his former Albion teammate Curtis Davies.

'I knew Curt from our days at West Brom together,' said Robinson. 'He's a fantastic player. It could be tough to keep him this summer.'

April 2014

Lee Clark described Paul Robinson's impending absence as a 'huge loss' to Birmingham City.

The captain will be suspended for Blues next three games – all of them at St Andrew's – after being booked in the 1–0 defeat at Nottingham Forest in April 2014. It was Robinson's 15th yellow card of the season.

'He's a huge loss. He's been excellent for us,' said Clark, who didn't blame the defender for trying to halt Ben Osborn, who had broke through in the 90th minute. 'He tried to tackle the guy. I'm not going to stop somebody in my team trying to tackle. I think he's been hard done by with a lot of the bookings because he's very competitive in today's game. In a tackle you will knock an opponent over. We're without him now so I need some of my other players to step up to the plate.'

Blues did nothing to ease their Championship relegation fears with the City Ground defeat. They gifted Forest what turned out to be the only goal after just 97 seconds. Matt Derbyshire scored it after Jonathan Spector gave the ball away needlessly. Clark was critical of not just such an error by a senior player like Spector, but by the general approach in the first half. Blues were much improved after the break.

September 2014

In the *Four Four Two* football magazine issue's special supplement entitled 'Season Preview 2014–15' each club is designated a 'Key Player' for Blues it was inevitably Paul Robinson: 'The heart-on-sleeve' captain and defender, now 35, is a model of the graft and determination needed to survive in this division (Championship), and will need to help galvanise a much-changed squad quickly to do it again.'

Bluenoses would not argue with the *Four Four Two* choice particularly after Robbo's influence on a day In May 2014 when Blues travelled to Bolton Wanderers for the last match of the season. Paul was back in the team after a three-match suspension following a 15th booking for what I believe was the only 'real' tackle at the City Ground, Nottingham.

Above Brian Howard escorts Paul off the City Ground pitch after
the realisation that he will miss the next three games in the fight
against relegation to Division One

Although the plaudits for the remarkable escape go quite rightly to Paul Caddis the influence of Robbo cannot go unrecognised. The day was recorded in a *Birmingham Mail* 16-page souvenir entitled THE GREAT ESCAPE, Colin Tattum writes, 'Blues came, Blues conquered and how they roared. Against all odds they somehow managed to pull off The Great Escape and stop the club from plunging into oblivion. Championship survival on the last day of the season will go down as a watershed moment in the history of Birmingham City FC. Had they dropped down to League One – and at one time it looked that a relegation day was a nailed-on certainty – one can only imagine the consequences. The supporters were only too aware of the precarious state of their beloved club. They've seen so much heartache over the years – last day relegations, Cup Final defeats, Play-off misery, the list goes on.

But with their brave faces, slick suits, waistcoats and flat caps, the Peaky Blinders travelled to Bolton in their droves. By 11.45am the away end was almost full voice. *Keep Right On* echoed around the stands as the Blues players warmed up – but what followed wasn't pretty. Their brief of not losing at the Reebok Stadium and then bettering the Doncaster Rover's result against Champions Leicester City looked like too much to ask. Even when news filtered through to the 3,800 travelling fans that the Foxes had taken the lead, Blues conceded later and were 2–0 down with 14 minutes to save their season.

Something quite incredible happened next.
Backed by one of the most passionate set of supporters that ground will ever see, Blues fought back with goals from Nikola Zigic and a 93rd minute equaliser from Paul Caddis. And so they staved off the drop … on goal difference!

For many the rest is a blur. For others there are unanswered questions – where did the six minutes of injury time come from? How did Neil Danns (Note: ex-Blues player) miss that one-on-one for Bolton? Did that just happen?

Of course it's all history now, but certainly not forgotten. The echoes of Blues' famous and fitting terrace chant are still ringing out in supporters ears. Replays of Lee Clark's passionate sprint and leap into the crowd continue to circulate around social networking sites. And now the dust has finally settled those who witnessed the drama unfold can look back on the momentous occasion and proudly say. 'I was there' (*Birmingham Mail* – Saturday 10 May 2014).

New Season

In the official match day programme *Blues News* for the opening Championship game of the 2013–14 season at home versus Watford on Saturday 3 August, Robbo featured in an article entitled 'ROBBO LEADS THE WAY'.

'I know what they're like. They're a passionate lot and when you're not playing well they let you know. You accept that, they pay good money to come and watch you so I'm not going to hide away from that. At the same time I always believe that as long as you give your best, and even if that's not good enough, if you come off sweating blood then the fans will respond to that.'

Such comments leave the impression that Robinson would be quite at home in another era, his rugged style and relentless work ethic straight from the old school of English defending. He's been fearless to a fault on occasions too, like when Gianfranco Zola's men last visited. Playing on through the pain he couldn't cope with the pace of Ikecha Anya as Watford chalked up a comfortable win. 'We didn't perform on the day and they outplayed us from start to finish,' he admits. 'I didn't have the best of games; I can hold my hands up and say that. I picked up an injury in the first-half but I didn't want to come off when I should have. That's the kind of person I am. I let the team and myself down because I should have admitted I was struggling. Maybe that result was a blessing in disguise though. It was time for a change, for me to get fit, regroup and fight my way back into the team.'

Being substituted for the first and only time in his Blues career so far, with the away side already in control hurt Robinson's pride. He returned as a makeshift centre-half and became a permanent fixture in that position as results improved dramatically towards the tail end of the season. With the change in formation during pre-season to 3-5-2 it looks like he will remain there, marshalling the defence.

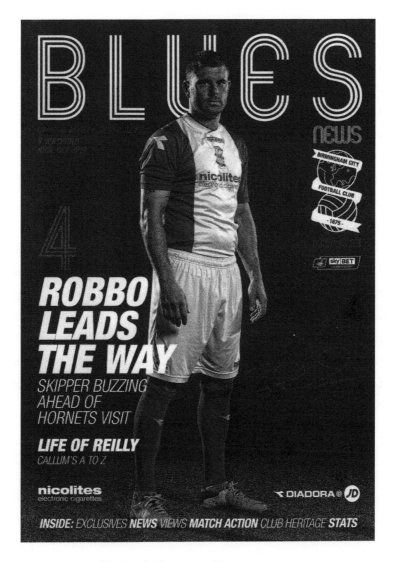

Robbo leads the way – Programme cover

'I see myself as a utility man from last year.' he laughs, 'I played all the way along the back four but wherever the gaffer asks me to play I'll go and give 100 per cent. Adjusting to the formation is going to take time because the players are still getting used to each other and how we communicate across the pitch. We've got to go out on the training pitch and work hard, then take that into a game.'

The preparation certainly reaped rewards against Hull in last weekend's final pre-season friendly, as goals from Andrew Shinnie and Matt Green secured victory. Today's opponents used a similar style to devastating effect last season and Robinson is anticipating another hard-fought contest with his hometown club. 'I always watch to see how Watford are getting on because it's where I was born and bred. It'll be a difficult game,' he adds. 'We know what they can do from last year, getting to the Play-off Final, and they'll be looking for promotion again.'

Robinson learned his trade with the Hornets, going on to make 250 appearances for the first team. And although he has many fond memories of his years at Vicarage Road, there is concern that their unusual transfer policy could be harming the very academy he came through. Last season they had 15 players on loan, most from the owner's other clubs, Udinese and Granada. Since the Football League voted to limit these numbers, several have been signed permanently instead.

'I think they've worked that loophole well,' he concedes. 'I'm disheartened by it. I was brought up through the youth system there and really enjoyed my time under Graham Taylor and Kenny Jackett, who's now the manager of Wolves. You always got your chance but I don't see that any more. I don't see the same opportunity for young lads who are working hard to get into the team.'

In contrast Blues are set to have several home-grown players involved on opening day and, as the big kick-off approaches, the experienced head charged with leading them out is keen to get going again. At 34 Robinson is as enthusiastic about the game as ever and determined that Blues will overcome adverse circumstances.

'I just get the buzz for football. It's what I love doing and I want to carry on until my legs tell me they've had enough,' he says 'I'm excited for the start of the season. It's a very tough league and, with the teams that are in it, this year's probably going to be the toughest out of any I've ever experienced. We've always got to stay positive though and go into each game believing we can take three points. The fans have seen this club go through a lot recently,' Robinson adds. 'We're looking to the future now, which is bright with all the new players we've got. I'd like them to have a little bit of patience because we are a young team and it's down to myself and the other senior players to bring it all together. Hopefully the fans will see that and get right behind us.'

MEMORABLE GAME 13

BIRM CITY 3 – BRISTOL ROVERS 0 • 14 January 2014

The FA Cup with Budweiser third round proper Venue:
St Andrews (Winners receive £67,500)

Birmingham City captain Paul Robinson netted his first goal in five years to help his side avoid an FA Cup upset against League Two side Bristol Rovers.

Far Post Header

Match Report:

Chris Burke also netted two goals as Lee Clark's side produced an impressive display at St Andrew's to set up a fourth round home tie against Swansea City. It was a night to remember for Robinson who last got his name on the score sheet back in 2009 when he scored for West Bromwich Albion, also in the FA Cup.

Blues had been forced to wait to play this third round tie following Bristol Rovers delayed replay win over Crawley Town in the last round.

But it did not affect their performance one bit and the Championship side showed they are determined to have a good run in the competition this season.

It could have been a different story if Rovers had taken the lead after just three minutes.

Elliott Richard was clean through on goal but he could only fire the ball straight at Birmingham keeper Colin Doyle.

Birmingham also had chances early in the game to open the scoring, but Rovers keeper Steve Mildenhall pulled off an amazing triple save to deny Paul Caddis and Lee Novak.

The deadlock was finally broken on 35 minutes when Shane Ferguson's deep corner eventually fell to Robinson who struck home from a narrow angle for his first goal of the season. Robinson could have added his second of the game after the break when he went on a long run into the Rovers half but saw his shot produce a fine save from Mildenhall.

Birmingham finally put the game beyond the visitors on 85 minutes when Burke got his first goal of the game after racing onto a through ball from Nikola Zigic. He kept his composure to fire the ball beyond Mildenhall. Burke added his second and Birmingham's third on 87 minutes when he struck a left foot shot into the corner of the net to line up a home tie against Premier League opposition in the next round.

Birmingham City: 13 Colin Doyle, 31 Paul Caddis, 8 Hayden Mullins, 4 Paul Robinson (Captain), 18 Mitch Hancox, 7 Chris Burke, 20 Olly Lee (34 Adams 89mins), 29 Reece Brown (15 Elliott 73mins), 27 Shane Ferguson (33 Gray 89mins), 12 Lee Novak, 19 Nikola Zigic.
Subs not used: 30 Townsend, 14 Packwood, 17 Reilly, 22 Shinnie.

Bristol Rovers: 1 Steve Mildenhall, 2 Michael Smith, 6 Tom Parkes, 29 Mark McChrystal, 4 Lee Brown, 15 Oliver Norburn (7 David Clarkson 76mins), 24 Ollie Clarke (4 Danny Woodards 76mins), 10 Eliot Richards, 32 John-Joe O'Toole, 17 Ellis Harrison (19 Chris Beardsley 63mins), 9 Matt Harrold.

Substitutes not used: 18 Mitch Harding, 20 Conor Gough, 30 Tom Lockyer, 34 Pat Keary.

Attendance: 9,914 • **Referee**: Tony Harrington.

MEMORABLE GAME 14

SHEFF WEDNESDAY 4 – BIRM CITY 1 • 15 March 2014

Sheffield Wednesday: Caolan Lavery 16 minutes and 68 minutes, Leon Best 21 minutes and Will Packwood (own goal) 58 minutes.

Birmingham City: Lee Novak 80 minutes.

Attendance: 20,637 • **Venue:** Hillsborough
• **Referee:** Stephen Martin.

Match Report:

Awful Blues were brushed aside by an eager and aggressive Sheffield Wednesday. It was a horror show worse than the defeat at Leeds United. Blues never seemed at the races and their performance was strewn with errors and poor defending. Two goals in five first-half minutes when the match was meandering along in scrappy fashion gave the home side the momentum. And they never looked back, scored twice more after the break.

Lee Novak scored a consolation with 10 minutes left but Blues were a well-beaten side by then. To compound matters, Paul Robinson was taken off at half-time after being knocked out – he initially insisted on carrying on. And Blues lost Emyr Huws through injury and had to play out the final 11 minutes with 10 men as all the substitutes had been used.

The opener came in the 16th minute when a long, diagonal pass by Kieran Lee sailed over Tyler Blackett. Caolan Lavery nipped back inside him too easily on the right of the area and then stuck a low left-footer past Darren Randolph to the far post. It was all so straightforward, just like Sheffield's next goal, from a corner by Chris Maguire on the right. He crossed the ball into the near post and Lavery, pulling off, was sharp ahead of Robinson and flicked goalwards. Randolph reacted and parried but the ball spun just a yard from the goalline on the turf and Leon Best had a simple task to prod it in.

Lee Clark was obviously not happy and substituted Blackett two minutes after the second goal. Paul Caddis came on and went to right-back and Jonathan Spector moved across to take Blackett's left-back position. Blues then began to make some headway and pass the ball but they could not break Sheffield's resistance.

In the 37th minute there was major concern when Robinson was knocked out after a clash of heads with Lavery. After he hit the deck he lay motionless and immediately the referee signalled for medical attention. Blues players crowded round their stricken skipper and it didn't look good. After four minutes' treatment Robinson got groggily to his feet and, spurning a stretcher, hobbled off, an arm draped round Dr Mike Stone for support.

Aaron Martin was stripped and ready to replace him but, remarkably, Robinson insisted on returning to the fray after a few moments composing himself on the side lines. Martin sat back down in the dugout and, as play resumed, the ball came straight to Robinson and he headed it away.

In first-half stoppage time Blues were fortunate not to concede a third goal when, from a Lewis Buxton cross on the right, Atdhe Nuhiu got his body in the way of Packwood and bounced him off then shot home from close range. But the referee ruled out the goal and Blues breathed a sigh of relief.

Perhaps inevitably, Robinson was substituted at half-time with Martin taking his place after all. Packwood made a key challenge to stop Nuhiu rumbling down on goal from the left just before Federico Macheda came on and Blues went to a 4-4-2. But it made no difference whatsoever as Blues cartwheeled to a heavy defeat. Sheffield scored their third in the 58th minute from a break down the left. Jeremy Helan bombed past Caddis and turned in a cross to the six-yard box. Packwood stuck out a leg to try to clear only for the ball to loop over him and drift over Randolph high into the net.

Sheffield could easily have had more. Huws gave the ball straight to Best, who was left one-on-one versus Martin. He tried to go outside him on the right but a well-timed tackle, on the slide, stopped a certain goal. Blues' best chance until Novak's goal came in the 63rd minute, but was messed up. Novak broke on the left and centred into the area, the ball bobbling all over the place. Chris Burke nudged it back to Andrew Shinnie 15 yards out but, off balance, he took a swipe and sliced wide.

Sheffield struck again, this time with a beauty. Blues were unable to clear their lines after a series of crosses and Maguire laid the ball back from the right for Lavery and he connected with a brilliant 25-yarder, a sweeping shot into the top corner on 68 minutes. Despite losing Huws, Blues then gained a small consolation when Novak registered on the scoresheet. Macheda drove into the area and delivered a fine ball to the far post and Novak darted in, slamming the ball home on the slide after 80 minutes.

Sheffield Wednesday: Damien Martinez, Lewis Buxton, Oguchi Onyewu, Sam Hutchinson, Glenn Loovens (Miguel Angel Llera 76 minutes), Kieron Lee, Jeremy Helan, Chris Maquire (Benik Afobe 69 minutes), Leon Best, Adthe Nuhise, Caolan Lavery (Yellow card 17 minutes, Jerome Johnson 81 minutes).
Substitutes Unused: Prutton, Davies, Cole and Palmer.

Birmingham City: Darren Randolph, Tyler Blackett (Paul Caddis 24 minutes), Jonathan Spector (Yellow card 65 minutes), Will Packwood, Paul Robinson (Aaron Martin 46 minutes), Tom Ademeyi, Andrew Shinnie, Chris Burke, Olly Lee (Frederico Macheda 58 minutes), Emyr Huws, Lee Novak.
Substitutes Unused: Ibe, Zigic, Rusniak and Doyle.

Player Profile:

Tyler Blackett was a local boy initially picked up by Manchester United at the age of eight in 2002 and he rose through the youth scheme earning a reputation as a strong and versatile centre-back also capable of playing at left-back and even on the left wing. In 2013–14, he spent short spells on loan at Blackpool and Birmingham City, in the Championship, for his first taste of professional football. Returning to Old Trafford, the 20-year-old was virtually unknown by the majority of United fans before this season. But he has now started all four Premier League games in the new campaign, looking very able and assured in each, much more so than the vastly more experienced Jonny Evans. A tall, physical and athletic player, Blackett operates in a similar way to former United star Rio Ferdinand. He reads the game very well and can break up attacks simply rather than by diving into tackles. He also possesses good ball control and excellent distribution, as well as being able to strike a free-kick.

On 31 January 2014, Blackett signed for Championship club Birmingham City on a youth loan until the end of the season. Together with fellow Manchester United loanee Tom Thorpe, Blackett started the next day's match, at home to Derby County. After 38 minutes, he tripped Will Hughes to concede a penalty, which Darren Randolph saved. Birmingham came back from 3–1 down to draw, the equaliser scored by a third United loanee, Federico Macheda, in stoppage time.

Birmingham City Boss boss Lee Clark has praised on-loan Manchester United defender Tyler Blackett after hooking him off against Sheffield Wednesday.

Clark made a change in only the 23rd minute, substituting left-back Blackett after Blues conceded two quick goals. 'I sat down with him on Monday and told him the reasons,' Clark revealed. 'I don't think it was the right time to speak to him on the day once I had made that decision. 'Tyler handled it really well. He handled it like a senior professional. 'We sat down and had a chat on Monday, I explained my reasons, I explained what I wanted from him. He understood and he is in contention for Reading. It's as simple as that. 'I have got to make these decisions sometimes.

'We did concede more than the two after Tyler came off but that was more down to bad luck because if my captain had still be on the pitch it wouldn't have gone to four, I'm convinced about that. 'But, you know, the early part of the game there were too many things happening that were causing me concern defensively.'

MEMORABLE GAME 15

BOLTON WANDERERS 2 – BIRM CITY 2 • 3 May 2014

Bolton Wanderers: Lee Chung-Yong 57 minutes, Lukas Jutkiewicz 76 minutes.

Birmingham City: Nikola Zigic 78 minutes, Paul Caddis 90 minutes.

Attendance: 19,558 • **Venue:** Reebok Stadium.
• **Referee:** Iain Williamson.

Match Report:

Blues clinched survival in the most dramatic fashion as Paul Caddis' header three minutes into stoppage time prevented the 2011 League Cup winners from dropping into the third tier of English football for the first time in 20 years. With 14 minutes remaining, second-half strikes from Bolton's Lee Chung-Yong and Lukas Jutkiewicz had left Lee Clark's men staring down the abyss.

Yet late goals from Nikola Zigic and Caddis earned them a 2–2 draw, and Leicester's win over Doncaster therefore meant Blues, who only dropped into the bottom three for the first time this season a week ago, stayed up at the expense of Doncaster.

It meant Clark's men, who were playing in the top flight just three seasons ago, can now look to rebuild. The club is reportedly up for sale after former owner Carson Yeung was sentenced to six years in prison for money laundering, while Clark and the future of many of his players, a handful of whom are on loan deals, remains murky.

Captain Paul Robinson was back in the Blues starting line-up following suspension and Clark recalled big-earning Zigic, probably for the final time before he is released this summer. He was involved in a bright opening patch for the visitors too with both him and Emyr Huws, the only loanee selected in Clark's XI, seeing shots blocked while Lee Novak was inches away from turning Caddis' driven cross home.

However, Birmingham failed to build on that spell and Wanderers came close with both Lee and Rob Hall narrowly missed the target with decent efforts. Clark's men would find a second wind before the break, though, and they kept Bolton's back-up goalkeeper Andy Lonergan busy. Twice he denied Novak with fingertip saves, the first in particular was a fine stop down to his left, and although the ex-Huddersfield forward eventually found a way past Lonergan, the whistle had already blown for Zigic's foul on David Wheater.

While Birmingham's need for victory was evident in their hurried play, the hosts were, perhaps understandably, far more ponderous with visiting goalkeeper Darren Randolph having little to do. As the two sides headed into the tunnel at half-time, Blues knew they were going down with Doncaster drawing and Millwall winning. Yet they were surprisingly slow out of the blocks and were punished for it 12 minutes after the restart.

David Wheater was given plenty of time to pick his pass into the box and Lee spun before rifling a finish into the far corner from the right-hand side of the area. Clark responded by introducing Jordan Ibe and Federico Macheda, both part of the second batch of Birmingham loanees who had come under fire from captain Robinson for a perceived lack of effort. Ibe at least gave them more directness out wide and Lonergan flipped the Liverpool winger's cross into Novak's path, but he could not bring the ball under his spell quickly and eventually smashed a low shot past the post.

Birmingham's attacking play got increasingly desperate and scrappy but their fans were heartened by news of a Leicester goal against Doncaster. They relayed the message that they now only needed one goal to their players but, as those chants sounded out, substitute Jutkiewicz doubled the hosts' advantage.

The Middlesbrough loanee picked up the ball on the left channel and somehow skewed a shot under Randolph's near post 14 minutes from time. However, two minutes later, Zigic gave the travelling support hope once more when he bundled the ball over the line after a cross from the left ended up in his path. Neil Danns should have restored Bolton's two-goal lead but blazed over the bar and with six additional minutes signalled, Birmingham had a chance.

And it was another mad sequence of events, which led to their all-important equaliser in the third of those half-a-dozen minutes added on. Zigic's header was cleared off the line by Tim Ream and the ball fell kindly for Caddis to nod in from barely a yard out and spark jubilant scenes in the stands and along on the touchline.

Bolton Wanderers: Andy Lonergan, Tim Ream, Oscar Threlkeld, Matthew Mills (Yellow card 61 minutes), David Wheater (Yellow card 70 minutes), Jay Spearing, Liam Trotter, Neil Danns, Lee Chung-Yong (Zat Knight 81 minutes), Rob Hall (Lukas Jutkiewicz 61 Minutes), Jermaine Beckford (Andy Kellett 86 minutes).

Birmingham City: Darren Randolph, Jonathan Spector, Paul Caddis (Yellow card 90 minutes), Hayden Mullins, Paul Robinson (Yellow card 56 minutes), Chris Burke (Jordan Ibe 60 minutes), Emyr Huws (Mitch Hancox 46 minutes), Callum Reilly (Frederico Maceda 60 minutes), Tom Ademeyi, Nikola Zigic (Yellow card 90 minutes) Lee Novak.

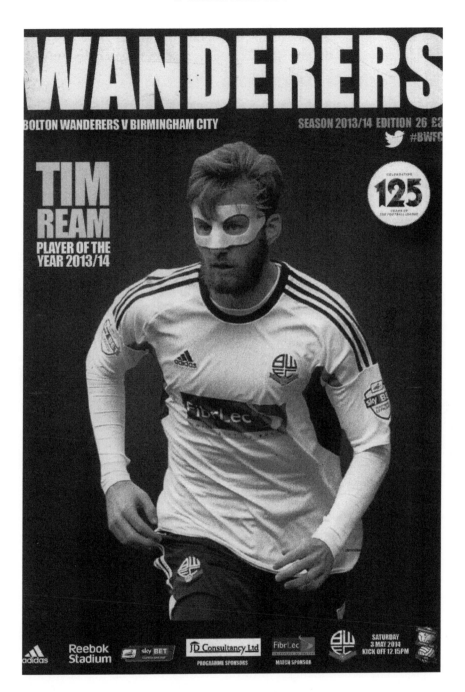

Bolton Programme Cover

MEMORABLE GAME 16

BIRM CITY 0 – BOURNEMOUTH 8 • 25 October 2014

Birmingham City: Randolph, Hall, Edgar (sent-off 7 minutes), Robinson, Grounds, Cotterill, Caddis, Gleeson (Reilly 45 minutes), Novak (booked 11 minutes, Arthur 66 minutes) Donaldson, Thomas (Davis 10 minutes).
Substitutes unused: Packwood, Shinnie, Shea and Doyle.

Bournemouth: Artur Boruc, Simon Francis, Tommy Elphick, Steve Cook, Charlie Daniels, Matt Ritchie, Harry Arter (Dan Gosling 56 minutes), Andrew Surman, Marc Pugh, Brett Pitman (Tokelo Rantie 64 minutes) and Callum Wilson (Ryan Fraser 71 minutes).

Attendance: 13,837 • **Referee:** Keith Hill.

Scorers: Pitman 3 minutes, Wilson 35 minutes, Ritchie 40 minutes, Pugh 63, 69 and 84 minutes, Rantie (pen) 82 and 86 minutes.

Marc Pugh scored three of Bournemouth's goals as the Cherries moved into the Championship play-off places. It could, indeed should, have been double figures: whoever takes over from the sacked Lee Clark as manager of Birmingham City, it can only be someone who has very little to lose. Which is probably why the former Manchester United assistant Mike Phelan is the favourite, ahead of the Burton Albion manager and the former Birmingham player Gary Rowett. Given the parlous state of the Blues, off and self-evidently on the field, Rowett, who is building a reputation as a promising young manager with the Brewers, might be well advised to steer well clear.

Eddie Howe, one can surmise, is unlikely to be among those to have sent in their CV. This was Bournemouth's fourth successive league victory, establishing them in a Championship play-off position, and while their lack of resources render their prospects of reaching the Premier League unlikely, the fact is that Howe – who is only 36 – has already guided them to two promotions thereby ensuring their challenge must be taken seriously.

Howe sounded almost nonplussed after seeing his side run up a record league win, and inflict a record home defeat on a Birmingham side reduced to 10 men after barely five minutes.

'We got a great start, with an early goal and then a sending off going in our favour, but we really put them to the sword in the second half. It's not always easy to exploit a numerical advantage – we were reduced to 10 for 60 minutes against Bolton ourselves recently and went on to win the game – but we went about it the right way, we didn't show any arrogance or disrespect, and some of our attacking play in the second-half was a joy to watch."

Not for the Birmingham fans it wasn't. It took all of three minutes for Bournemouth to go ahead, when the City defenders Paul Robinson and Jonathan Grounds stood and waited for each other to make a tackle on Brett Pitman, allowing the forward to run through unopposed before sliding the ball under the advancing goalkeeper Darren Randolph. A Sunday league side would have been ashamed.

Three minutes later a dithering David Edgar allowed Callum Wilson to bully him out of possession before blatantly tugging his shirt. With no one between Wilson and Randolph, it was no surprise to see the referee Keith Hill show Edgar the red card.

The atmosphere in St Andrew's, already gloomy, sank further when Randolph – not for the first time – scuffed a clearance kick. Matt Ritchie played the ball back through to Wilson (who looked well offside) and the forward rounded Randolph and scored.

Five minutes later Ritchie was the beneficiary. Robinson was again at fault, hitting an attempted clearance straight at the Bournemouth midfielder, who ran on to the rebound and lobbed the stranded Randolph.

Offered a chance to put the Blues on the scoreboard eight minutes into the second half after Tommy Elphick had fouled Clayton Donaldson, Paul Caddis failed to beat the Bournemouth goalkeeper Artur Boruc from the spot, and Birmingham's pain only increased as Marc Pugh acrobatically volleyed the visitor's fourth, before heading their fifth, in both cases from crosses by Simon Francis.

The substitute Tokelo Rantie made it six from the spot, before Pugh completed his hat-trick, turning home a cross-shot and Rantie made it eight.

'What can I say?' asked the Birmingham co-caretaker manager Malcolm Crosby. 'In the end it was an embarrassment. I don't blame the circumstances. A couple of things went against us, but there can be no excuses for losing 8–0. Even when we got a penalty we missed it. It's been a terrible day and we apologise to the supporters.'

This defeat went down in the history of Birmingham City Football Club as the biggest home defeat in its 139-year history and Robbo was captain. He showed the qualities of a captain by two actions: a) He ensured the players remained on the pitch after the final whistle to applaud the fans, who had been defiant and sang *Keep Right On to The End of the Road* even when the fifth goal went in! Although as the goals continued to go in a section of the crowd turned on the players with chants of 'you're not fit to wear the shirt', Robbo ensured the players did not hide and faced the boos of criticism. This action drew some criticism from Kevan Broadhurst who was commentating on the match alongside Tom Ross on Free Radio 80. Broadhurst, a previous captain of the Blues, said that he would have been too ashamed to go and applaud the fans after such a performance and would have left the pitch in a hurry. Interestingly different approach to the role of a captain; b) He made a post-match apology via video on the Blues' web site saying he vowed that the players would work hard to make amends, 'I can only apologise to the fans for that shambles of a game. We're all very disappointed; the fans will be even more disappointed paying lot of money to come and watch – that is not acceptable. We all know we have got to knuckle down as a team and work hard. When you lose 8–0 you don't forget it but I'm not going to stand here and throw the towel in because I'm not that kind of person. I'm going to get the lads together and we're going to put this right together. This group can recover, because they're a good bunch of lads. They're going to take full responsibility, like I have. They are going to get on the training ground on Monday and get ourselves ready for Wolves. If the new manager does come in, then I think he has had a bit of a wake-up call with players he has got to work with. But when he sees the players he will know they are a good group of lads."

For the record Blues went to Molineux the following Saturday with Gary Rowett in charge and secured a 0–0 draw.

Robbo with 100 shirt!

NEWS

DAVE'S EZE WISH COMES TRUE

A chance to meet Paul Robinson eased the disappointment of Blues' hefty home defeat by AFC Bournemouth for fan and cancer sufferer Dave Roberts.

Thanks to an EZE Wish granted by Blues diamond partner EZE Group, Dave, from Solihull, had a post-match chat with the club captain. The 66-year-old lifelong Blues fan, who has incurable bowel cancer, had just witnessed the club's eight-goal thrashing at St. Andrews, but his spirits were boosted by his encounter with the amiable defender.

"Meeting Paul did lift my mood somewhat", said Dave. "And I thought it was very brave of him to come and face everyone like that after such a heavy defeat. It takes someone like the club captain to do that. We had a good chat, and I reminded him that we'd met some years ago, when he played for Watford. I used to be a season

ticket holder, but this was the first game I've been to this season, and would you believe it – it was an 8-0 drubbing! It was a great day in the EZE Group box though, and the hospitality shown by Blues was superb."

EZE Group's Gary Smith said: "The last thing many players would want to do after a result like that, especially at home, is chat to fans. But Paul's such a great guy; he was only too happy to meet Dave, and hearing about his battle with cancer certainly put the match into perspective for him."

Dave was nominated for an EZE Wish by Shirley Golf Club pal Gerry Clarke.

Blues fans are urged to write to ezewishes@bcfc.com nominating fellow fans who they feel deserve an EZE Wish. These are considered on a regular basis, and the most deserving wishes are granted.

EZE Group's Gary Smith and Blues fan Dave Roberts meet skipper Paul Robinson.

ROBBO'S CENTURY

Meanwhile, the Blues skipper is on the verge of chalking up a significant milestone today. If, as expected, Robinson features in this afternoon's game against Cardiff City then it will be his 100th appearance for the club.

The Watford-born centre-half moved to St. Andrew's in September 2012 and has been a mainstay of the Blues backline ever since. The evergreen defender, who turns 36 next month, signed a new one-year contract last summer.

Robinson is set to clock up his Blues century today.

Robbo 100 signature

The Birmingham Mail, 9 January 2015, reported by Brian Dick

Midfield dynamo David Davis has revealed Paul Robinson's part in helping Blues recover from one of the worst defeats in club history. The midfielder, who has since emerged as a key part of Gary Rowett's team, has described how the club captain rallied the troops after the 8–0 hammering by Bournemouth in October.

That loss came in the final match before Rowett took over at St Andrew's, since when Blues have won six times and hauled themselves out of the relegation zone and into mid-table. Much has been written about Rowett's enormous contribution, but it has emerged that Robinson also wanted to draw a line in the sand by calling a team meeting. 'After the Bournemouth game we had a meeting between ourselves and said, "Look, we are not in a bad position",' Davis said. 'I think we were 13 or 14 games in then so we said "We just needed to step up and be counted, man up and be mentally tough". We all knew the new manager was coming in so we needed to be mentally tough for him and the whole of Birmingham City because obviously that was not a good day. We felt like we let everyone down, for us it was about bouncing back. Paul Robinson pulled us to one side and we had a meeting between ourselves. We felt that was what was needed before the manager came in to look for a fresh start for everyone.

'He just basically said, "We have got to stand up and be counted and put this behind us, we can't remember it because if we do we won't get out of the position we are in." I think everyone has reacted to that, it was a positive meeting we haven't looked back.'

Indeed not, Davis and Robinson have played every game since then and Blues have improved both their home record and their clean sheet ratio – failings that seriously undermined them before Rowett's arrival.

And Davis was also fulsome in his praise of the Birmingham manager. 'I can't speak highly enough of him,' he said. 'He has shown faith in me; he has just let me express myself and play my football. He is obviously a young manager with a very good future ahead of him. He has shown he is a good manager, he is positive in everything he does. His style of football is working for him and it's rubbing off on every team he's been at.'

Lots of challenges and passion

'I always believe in my own ability, believe in the type of character I am, as club's always need players like myself who are out there. I kept working hard in training by myself and you've just got to keep at it. You've got a wife and kids at home to supply for and I've just got to keep pushing myself. Sometimes I push myself to limits I didn't even know I had and that's just the nature of who I am. My agent phoned me and said, "Birmingham have had a lot of injuries at the back and they'd like to have a look at you", so straight away I came down.'

It was a chance for Paul to work with a manager who has similar traits as himself in Lee Clark. Both men are renowned for their passion and determined attitudes towards every game.

'He achieved so much as a player and played for some amazing clubs and has taken that over to management. It's a big step and people have to respect what goes on behind the scenes. There has been a lot to deal with since he has been at the club and he is doing a fantastic job. The manager can only pick eleven players and it's up to us to perform well. He's pretty similar to other managers really. He has Bryan Robson's passion, Graham Taylor's tactical awareness and ways of dealing with pressure, Gianluca Vialli's love of technique and possession based training. So he blends into all of them really and he's still young and improving. In the future he could manage one of the top sides in the country.

'If anything, Stephen was the biggest departure from the dressing room because of the character he was and the aura he had around the dressing room. I wish I could have been in the same team as him, but for him to pass that armband onto me was a great feeling. It's a challenge with all the changes we've had since the summer due to all the new faces in the team, so for me to lead the team and keep the atmosphere bubbling is great.

'The young lads at Blues (Reece Brown, Mitch Hancox, Callum Reilly, Dimi Gray et al) can go a long way. If they keep their feet on the ground, keep listening to the right players and not getting influenced by people that know nothing about football. These players are now in a great position at this club to come through and show what they can do. It's like when I was at Watford because they'll all come through together and hopefully not get influenced by others and the money in the game.'

BIRMINGHAM MAIL FOOTBALL ANNUAL 2013–2014
THE SKIPPER by COLIN TATTUM

Paul Robinson may be reaching the autumn of his years. But he is enjoying his football as much as ever. And that, for the Blues' captain, is a key component for the whole squad this coming season.

Robinson, 34, joined Blues in an emergency as a free agent in September on a month's contract, to cover for injuries. Thirty-seven games and the skipper's armband later, he is an integral part of Lee Clark's young side.

'It was strange, the way I came to the club, and it was great challenge,' reflects the former Albion stalwart. 'When you think your last game is coming up, you look forward to it. You go and enjoy yourself and just have fun. It continued right through the season for me like that. I had one month (contract), two months and then gradually it was extended until the end. It brought the best out of me, my character, and as a person it made me stronger. And obviously from a coach's point of view, it was great encouraging and helping the young lads at the same time. I thoroughly enjoyed every part of it. And it's going to be the same this season. Yes you have got to go out there and be a professional, do what you have to do. But you have also got to enjoy yourself – that's important for all of us.'

Robinson signed a new one-year contract with a year's option, in the summer and Clark installed him as Curtis Davies' replacement as captain. He did the UEFA B Coaching badge and plans to move into that field, or management when he hangs up his boots. Whilst that may still be a couple of years off, Robinson's knowledge and the example he sets around Wast Hills will be tapped into once more. Clark wants it that way, and so does Robinson – and the 'Junior Blues' as he joking calls the youngsters. 'I look after myself and I'll know when enough is enough and then hopefully go into the coaching and management side of things,' said Robinson. 'But it won't be just yet. Yes, we have got a lot of younger players and there is a responsibility on me and the other more experienced lads to help them in any way we can. You have to. You are a senior pro;

you have to set an example. You are always there for them to talk to you about what's wrong, or how they are doing. It gives them a lift – as well as yourself – knowing that they can come and talk to you to see what your point of view is.' Robinson excelled at centre-half in the last 11 games of the previous season keeping Steven Caldwell out of the side. 'I think the only place I haven't played is up front, so I will ask to start there and work my way back!' he joked.

About his lack of height, Robinson who played in the back three at Watford commented. 'I think at any club you're at, people look at that physicality for a centre-half, but it is also about having a football brain, knowing your positioning, when to get tight, when to drop off. Alongside Curtis Davies, I think it was the best football I'd played all season. Wherever the manager plays me, I will give my best. And if I am not playing, I'd still be doing all I can to help the boys.'

Pre-season 2014–15
25 July 2014.
Lee Clark is reported in the local press:

'Of the two who are a little bit short of action, Jonathan Spector (groin) and Paul Robinson (knee during the pre-season tour of Ireland) we haven't been able to get them back on the training pitch as yet. Certainly with Paul it is about keeping him right for the season, 10 months not the next ten days, which is something we've had a conversation about. His training programme was always going to be modified. He's the oldest member of the squad, it's about getting him out on the pitch as much as possible, it's not about getting training ground minutes into Paul. He is aware of that and the medical team are, so we're quite cool with that one.'

Loan Players

The financial restraints imposed on Birmingham City by its imprisoned owner meant that Lee Clark was forced to use the loan system to create a team that could compete at Championship level. The initial loan players were impressive but Captain Paul Robinson says the Championship strugglers' current group of loanees have let them down. Robinson said: 'The first batch of loan players were different class, buying into the gaffer's ethos and that of the team and what we expected from each other. For me the second lot (those signed in 2014) have let us down a little bit.'

Lee Clark's reputation enabled him to attract young players from top Premier League sides such as Manchester City. Manchester United and Liverpool but as good as the contribution was from the first batch, the second group failed to contribute at the same level.

Defender Robinson added, 'You don't want anyone out there now not giving 100%. The players that go our there have got to wear the shirt with pride.' The City skipper is currently serving a three-match suspension after receiving 15 yellow cards this season (2013–14) Blues lie 21st in the Championship, above the relegation zone on goal difference. Since the end of the January transfer window, 12 of Blues' 21 league goals have been scored by loan players, including nine for striker Macheda, now the club's top league goalscorer this season. 'The big clubs send these players out for a reason and that's to get first-team football,' 35-year-old Robinson continued. 'For me, they've let the gaffer down, they've let us players down, some of them, and they'll just go back to their clubs and get on with it. That hurts me the most because we're football players and we're brought up to love the game. Do these young kids love the game as much? I don't think so.' Previous loanees, Jesse Lingard from Manchester United scored six goals in thirteen appearances, whilst Dan Burn

(Fulham) and Kyle Bartley (Swansea City) formed an impressive back four pairing enabling the club to enjoy a 10-match unbeaten run. Manager Lee Clark added, 'Every Loan player that's come here has the ability. That's not the point in what we're saying, all the first batch bought into Birmingham City. In the second batch we've had some who have done that as well, but there have been others who failed to respond appropriately.'

The table below shows my season-by-season appearances for the St Andrew's club:

SEASON	LEAGUE	FA CUP	LEAGUE CUP	OTHER	TOTAL
2012–23	35(0)	2(0)	0(0)	0(0)	37(0)
2013–14	40(0)	2(1)	4(0)	0(0)	46(1)
2014–15	22(3)		1		23(3)

Note: The publisher's deadline to receive the final draft of *ROBBO – UNSUNG HERO* is mid-January with Paul's footballing career continuing it is worth noting that at the end of 2014 his Career Total reads as: 596 League appearances (12 goals) 40 FA Cup appearances (2 goals) 27 League Cup appearances (1 goal) 8 Other appearances (0 goals) TOTAL 671 appearances (15 goals).

7.

'Reflections'

Writing a book like this with a co-writer like Keith has enabled me to record some of the thoughts and memories I have as I reach my 37th year and nearly 20 years in the game:

- My feeling is that FA Cup semi-finals should not be played at Wembley, that experience should be restricted to the Final only. I would like to go back to the days when semi-finals were played on a neutral ground with equal travelling distances for both sets of fans e.g. Hillsborough, Villa Park, Goodison Park etc.

- If I could select a team from the best eleven players I have played with during my career, that team would be:

Dean Kiely	(West Bromwich Albion 2007–2011)
Nigel Gibbs	(Watford 1983–2002)
Gary Cahill	(Bolton Wanderers 2008–2012)
Jonas Olsson	(West Bromwich Albion 2008 – Current)
David Murphy	(Birmingham City 2008–2014)
Lee Cheung-Yong	(Bolton Wanderers 2009 – Current)
Jack Wilshere	(Bolton Wanderers – Loan – 2010)
Jonathan Greening	(West Bromwich Albion 2004-2010)
Zoltan Gera	(West Bromwich Albion 2004–2008 and 2011–2014)
Kevin Phillips	(See Foreword on Page 7)
Daniel Sturridge	(Bolton Wanderers – Loan – 2011)

- If I could select a team from the best eleven players I have played against during my career, that team would be:

Edwin Van Der Sar
Gary Neville
John Terry
Sol Campbell
Ashley Cole
David Beckham
Robbie Keane
Cristiano Ronaldo
Ryan Giggs
Paul Scholes
Alan Shearer or Ruud van Nistelroy

- The eleven best players in my position are in my opinion in no particular order

Paolo Cesare Maldini
Franco Berasi
Ashley Cole
Michael Cavallaro
John Terry
Stuart Pearce
Mats Hummels
Vincent Kompany
Leighton Baines
Jamie Garragher

My mentors
As I have expressed elsewhere in my book I have a burning desire to stay in the game either in a management or coaching role, although I do not see

myself as a television or radio pundit it might be that I need to do that in the short-term to keep my name on the radar when jobs become available.

As well as obtaining my coaching badges/licences to the highest possible level and therefore being technically proficient, I would want to pass on the lessons I have learnt during my career from some of the great managers who have helped my development as a footballer: Kenny Jackett, Graham Taylor, Gianluca Vialli and Ray Lewington at Watford – Gary Megson at West Bromwich Albion and Bolton Wanderers – Bryan Robson and Tony Mowbray at West Bromwich Albion and Owen Coyle at Bolton Wanderers. Beside their individual attributes each of them demonstrated to me that to get the best results on the field you need players who have skill together with the right attitude. A player with 50% skill and 50% of the right attitude will always serve a team better than a player with 100% skill and the wrong attitude. (Note: Sir Clive Woodward won the Rugby Union World Cup with England using the equation – PERFORMANCE = CAPABILITY x ATTITUDE[2]

- Lee Clark – he gave me a chance to extend my playing career and I will always be grateful for that, as my time at Birmingham has been a wonderful extension to my career having made over 100 appearances. Although I did not get the chance to say goodbye to him face-to-face we have spoken subsequently and I wish him well at Blackpool. So from Lee I have learnt that you judge a player by what he can do on the pitch for your team and nothing else.

- Gary Rowett – when he and his team arrived at the Wast Hills Training Ground only a few days before the lunchtime fixture at Wolverhampton scheduled for 1 November 2014, the first thing they did was to speak with me as Senior Pro and club/team captain. They asked me for my views on the club, team and recent experiences and they listened and gave consideration to my comments. So from Gary I have learned that to train at match intensity is physically demanding, but gets results and the need to create a loyal team around you. Gary has three ex-Blues players in the team, which he brought with him as part of his move from Burton Albion and they get on great with each other and the players. The atmosphere is professional but done with a smile and a bit of banter and they do not take themselves too seriously. Training under Gary has changed, as well as the match intensity point; he also preaches to the players there must be a mutual individual trust between manager and player. The routine is varied, changing on a day-by-day basis; days off are not fixed although training days normally run from 10.30 to 12.00 (11.30 on Fridays). For away matches we tend to meet at Wast Hills on a Friday at 18.00 hours, have something to eat and then head off to our overnight hotel.

Club Finances

At two of my clubs I have played with financial problems occurring in the background: Watford and Birmingham City.

At Watford it was reported on 14 June 2002 that Ray Wilkins had been made redundant along with Giovanni Vaglini (Fitness Coach), John Kelly (Masseur) and Club Doctor Ian Beasley. Vialli kept his job but did not agree with the decisions made by the Chief Executive, Tim Shaw. It was grim times for us following the Carlton-Granada Digital TV debacle, which left the club with a £6m shortfall. The players did what they could by agreeing to deferred payments on their wages. The freehold to Vicarage Road was sold on 9 August 2002 for £6m plus an annual rent income of £630k. Although you try and ignore what is going on behind the scenes you cannot stop seeing the newspaper coverage and what's being discussed on the radio, the television and by the supporters.

The Birmingham City scenario is more recent and a lot more complicated due to the club's ownership by Birmingham International Holdings Limited, which is listed on the Hong Kong stock market. After the takeover by Carson Yeung the club experienced a League Cup victory over Arsenal at Wembley followed by relegation from the Premier League. Premier League status meant everything to the Chinese owners and a lack of enthusiasm for Championship status combined with an arrest and ultimate imprisonment for money laundering meant there was no investment in trying to regain Premier League status and many of the quality youngsters were sold to balance the books. A certain stability has been achieved this season but we are still limited in financial ambition to retaining our Championship status.

Watt Nicoll

I am currently reading *Twisted Knickers & Stolen Scones* by the motivational speaker and Personal Reinvention Expert Watt Nicoll. He has advised David Beckham as an individual but also worked with global brands such as Coca Cola, Heinz and Johnson & Johnson.

His own brand of persistence and determination alongside the fact that he has developed a process of self-education and self-awareness that has distinguished him as a world-class resource for the development of human potential. He has helped some of the world's most successful organisations and individuals achieve maximum performance such as English Football Association, Everton Football Club, Fulham Football Club, Scottish Football Association, Chris Coleman, Craig Brown, Wayne Rooney and David Moyes.

Watt Nicoll states;

'Believing that most of the truly accepted books on motivation and personal development have been based on the great American dream, I wrote this book for the purpose of awakening the unique Scottishness which sleeps deep within so many and, when awakened, has been so powerful in energising some of the greatest achievers in history. Recently I was given a great deal of interest from the media because I used some of the techniques from the book to assist the English football team and the Polish team did not find the results at all humorous. I do favour humour as a motivational tool!'

Ciaran Cosgrave

Paul's interest in Motivation began at Watford in *The Evening Standard* on Monday 7 June 1999 in which there was an article entitled 'Mr Motivator' – We introduce Watford's most recent signing and reveal his crucial role in the march to promotion.' David Bonds reports;

Flip charts, hurling and American psychology – believe it or not they all played a part in Watford's promotion to the Premiership. While attention focussed on the efforts of former England manager Graham Taylor and his team of cut-price players, one man's contribution went largely unnoticed. The timing of Dublin-born Ciaran Cosgrave's arrival at Vicarage Road suggests his role in Watford's return to the top flight merits some scrutiny.

Motivator Cosgrave, who learned his skills from two sports psychologists in America, wrote to Taylor at the turn of the year offering his services and explaining that he felt the Hertfordshire side, although doing better that expected, were still underachieving.

Three months later, following Taylor's recovery from a life-threatening throat complaint. Cosgrave was given the chance to prove what he could do. Now, three months after his appointment, Watford's players are on holiday before beginning preparations for their first season in the Premiership.

So just what did he say to Taylor's players to help them squeeze into the First Division Play-off Final where they played great football to beat Bolton Wanderers and earn a place in the big time? 'I told them on the Friday before that we weren't just going to Wembley, we were going there to win. There is a massive difference. When I first met the players they were ninth in the table and the first game I was involved with, a draw with Bury, was a huge disappointment. After that game I spoke to the players on my own and I simply asked them what they wanted. I then showed them some coverage of a hurling game in Ireland with the sound on the television turned down. I asked them to comment on it and they told me that thought they were all violent lunatics but they were amazed by the level of commitment when it was clearly so dangerous. I then told them that not one single player on that pitch was paid. You could have heard a pin drop. The next time they played at Tranmere they were 1–0 down but fought back and won 2–1 and we had two players sent off. It was the first time Watford had had a player sent off all season and it was the first time Graham had had two players sent off in one game in the whole of his career. But I think the message had got through. For the rest of the season they were so hungry and that's why we beat Bolton. We were much hungrier than them on the day. Bolton can say they were hungry, but it certainly didn't show.' Taylor said 'Ciaran has helped the players to look at themselves positively. Ever since I came back to the club I have been on to the players that it is all about mental fitness. You can be as physically fit as you like but if it isn't right between the ears, it is no good.'

8.

'The Game Today'

I have been asked many times my opinion on subjects which matter to those involved in the game whether in a professional capacity or as a fan. So here goes in reply to the question 'What do you think about…?'

FOREIGN PLAYERS

They have taken the English game to a higher level in terms of skill, which is great for everyone whether you are watching at the grounds or on the television. On the negative side I believe that the incredibly high wages foreign players command has taken a lot of money out of the game, which could have been invested in the grassroots development of the game.

Also their attitude can be poor. As I have described elsewhere in the book, for me attitude in all players is a key factor in success and therefore when some foreign players seem to come into the English game just for the money then it creates a negative attitude, which is not good for everyone involved.

I do not necessarily blame the introduction of foreign players for the situation whereby young English players are not coming through the system to get into the first team. I believe that the foreign players involvement could reduce opportunity and therefore is a factor but the main reason for the failure of the youth development system is a mixture of the standard of coaching – is it personalised enough to the individual player? And our attitude to the development into first team football, which is being helped by the introduction of Under 18 and Under-21 sides which give young players and squad professionals competitive football.

TACKLING – A LOST ART?

Well the days of the sliding tackle and the tackle from behind have gone and good riddance too. But the tackle must remain part of our game. We have all been to games when a tackle has excited the fans, got the team on the up and in some cases turned the game around.

The current thinking by referees and players is that if you go into a tackle with your studs showing then that is a foul and there will be consequences!

My only thought in terms of making a tackle is "Can I win the ball?" if I think I can win the ball then I will make a challenge. It is at that point that the assessment of the referee comes into play and sometimes they will get it wrong, as they are only human. Throughout my career I have witnessed situations where I have been judged by one referee to have fouled an opponent, which I know would not have happened with a different official. Consistency is required by everyone but it is an impossible dream because referees are individuals.

Another impact of the introduction of foreign players to the English game is that they have introduced the skill (if it is one?) of winning a free-kick. Whether it is described as simulation or diving I do not care but it makes me mad and on a numerous of occasions I have witnessed players who I know are cheating and conning the officials.

VIDEO TECHNOLOGY

I think it is a good idea as it helps referees make the right decisions, but it must be quick and enable the game to flow naturally. Hopefully we will never emulate Rugby Union whereby the game comes to a halt as the technology makes a decision.

The current goal line technology in the Premier League is great and should eventually go into all professional leagues as it is definitely an improvement to the game if those 'Is it a goal?' moments are objectively assessed.

SPORTS SCIENCE

I love it as it is keeping me playing!

When we are training all the players wear heart rate monitors, which are strapped, to our chests. On the odd occasion I have worn a GOPRO camera system, which records everything we do in a session that is incredibly helpful to the coaches and the individual players.

The old orange at half-time and a cup of tea have long since gone as we now get things like Recovery Shakes which are protein based, specific drinks and gels to overcome dehydration. As long as it keeps me playing longer I will try anything!

ROTATION SYSTEM

I accept it as part of the modern game but of course I want to play in every game! Still if it is handled and managed correctly then players accept it.

I was recently 'rotated' along with Clayton Donaldson, David Davis and Stephen Gleeson for the FA Cup third round tie for Birmingham City away at Blyth Spartans – a team 120 places below us in the leagues!

The gaffer told me immediately after the previous league match at Nottingham Forest in private and I fully understood his reasoning, but it was a game made for me! But in truth I enjoyed the rest (Hang On I took the family to Alton Towers so no rest there!).

It is not always about the individual, Gary Rowett had inherited a big squad from Lee Clark and because he had only used about the same 13 players for the last six games he has not had a chance to see a number of the squad members in action. As the game coincided with the January transfer window it was vital that Gary made decisions on players, based on seeing them play!

Just for the record, fielding a "rotated" team can come with some risks – at half-time Blues were losing 2–0 to the non-league club but fortunately the job was done 2–3 and we progressed into the fourth round.

YOUTH DEVELOPMENT

In 1999 The Football League and The FA Premier League produced a 16-page brochure entitled *Introducing the Football Academies*. In the section 'What happens when the student leaves school?' I contributed the following: 'The great thing about this game is that there is always the chance that one day your wildest dreams will come true. But you learn, as well, that the real world is out there. That's why the courses and study opportunities are so good in football'.

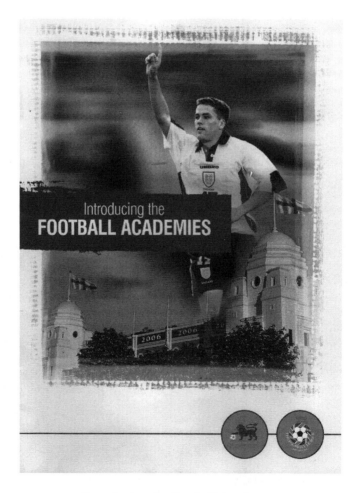

Introducing the Football Academies

FOOTBALL ADMINISTRATION

The Premier League should be more geared to supporting football rather than just their own members. You see now that the National Team is only selected from Premier League clubs it is too narrow a focus.

Bearing in mind the major changes in the ownership of football clubs in recent years, the Football League's Owners and Directors Test appeared to be a welcome introduction of a way to ensure that the owners and potential owners of football clubs were fit and proper people to run those businesses.

Unfortunately it would seem based on the Leeds United scenario regarding Massimo Cellino that the system has not been as effective as one would have hoped.

The Football Association should take more control on the wages paid to young players as "too much too soon" has resulted in a lot of failed football careers!

WHAT FIVE THINGS WOULD YOU DO TO IMPROVE THE GAME?

1) THE FOURTH OFFICIAL TO BE MORE INVOLVED WHAT IS HAPPENING ON THE PITCH!
At the moment the Fourth Official seems to indicate additional time and take the brunt of both manager's anger regarding decisions made by the referee. On rare occasions (and they are rare) they will intervene when a referee has made the wrong decision – a recent Birmingham City home game against Nottingham Forest resulted in the Fourth Official changing the referee's decision from a corner to Blues to a penalty! (See Chapter Ten.)

2) HAVE A WINTER BREAK
Every other European league has one so immediately it would put us on an equal footing for European and International tourna-

ments. It would also enable players to rest at a crucial time of the season. No longer is the justification for a break the condition of pitches in the winter, but one of making sure we are as competitive as possible in all competitions.'

3) CHANGE THE OFFSIDE RULE

Just reduce the complications and make it clear and simple for all.

4) PLAYER HEALTHCARE

The Football Association need to ensure that player's health is top of its agenda. Head Injuries are considered more appropriately these days thanks to the "Justice for Jeff" campaign (Jeff Astle – West Bromwich Albion striker 60s–70s who it is believed suffered dementia due to excessive heading of a football throughout his career). We need more regular and more rigorous health checks over and above the heart monitoring checks we currently get.

5) GET RID OF THE TRANSFER WINDOW

Get rid of the transfer window and allow transfers all year long with definite restrictions. These restrictions could be: Only a limited number of transfers allowed per year (as with the current Loan System) – A quota system for foreign and British footballers e.g. 50/50 throughout the year.

INJURIES

Throughout my career I have been very lucky with injuries – touch wood! Although bizarrely I have failed two medicals. The circumstances are interesting and somewhat different to what was reported in the press (See Chapter Four).

I was at The Albion and failed tests at Sunderland and Wigan Athletic.

Sunderland:

I failed the test because I have no anterior cruciate ligament (ACL) in my right knee. ACL is a tough band of tissue joining the thigh bone to the shin bone at the knee joint. It runs diagonally through the inside of the knee and gives the knee joint stability. It also helps control the back-and-forth movement of the lower leg. Apparently according to the Sunderland medical officer the fact that I had no ACL in my knee was due to an operation. I have never had an operation on the knee and if I had, I would have been out of the game for about nine months, but my playing statistics showed that no such absence has existed, plus there would have been medical records on my file and a scar.

Roy Keane was the manager at the time and it was in the close season which coincided with Caroline's 30th birthday and I had planned a weekend trip to Rome. We had just landed and were in the taxi on the way to our hotel when my agent called me, I thought he was joking, but sadly not, he had been notified that I was to get on the next available plane to the North East for a second medical with a specialist. It obviously disturbed the trip for both of us, but we had to see the bigger picture, it was potentially a great career move for me and Kevin Phillips had fully endorsed Sunderland as a good club. However the result of the medical was not good as the specialist had declared that my injury was career threatening as my knee would "explode" within two years!'

Wigan:

I was talking to Steve Bruce (remember what Brucie thought of me when he was at Birmingham City?), at the same time as Roy Keane and he would have heard about my failed medical through the football network but his doctor failed me due to a "back injury". I have never had a problem with my back throughout my life.

It would seem that I have never had ACL in my right knee from birth but one way or the other it resulted in my not moving from the Hawthorns.

This debacle obviously put silly things into my head and Tony Mowbray allowed me and Caroline to independently investigate these issues further with force plate testing and an independent knee and back specialist in London. All tests came back clear and I knew then I could focus on my game without any mental blocks about my body.

Well here we are seven years later and I am still playing professional football at a high level.

DISCPLINARY SYSTEM

At every match there is a Football Association appointed independent assessor and the question I have is, what does he do for me or any other player?

If I, as a player, make a bad decision in the game, which results in some disciplinary action, he records it and ultimately I get a ban and a fine as stipulated by the FA and the individual club rules. However if a referee makes a bad decision, which may have fundamentally affected the outcome of the game, there is no sanction that is applied, plus he does not even have to justify his actions in anyway shape or form.

REFEREES

Lee Clark as reported in the local press:

'He Knows What He Said' – Birmingham Boss Lee Clark Accuses Referee of Mocking His Player About Scoreline

Birmingham City manager Lee Clark has accused the referee who oversaw his side's dramatic 3–3 draw against Burnley at St. Andrews last night of teasing one of his players about the score line after the Blues went 2–1 down shortly after the hour mark.

If Clark is to be believed, referee James Linington mocked Birmingham captain Paul Robinson after booking him for dissent in the aftermath of Burnley's second goal of the evening, which came about when the Clarets were awarded a debatable free-kick just outside the Blues' area after Robinson had tangled with striker Danny Ings.

Clark, who was running a little high on emotion throughout the tie, told reporters after the game: 'There was an incident involving Danny Ings and Paul Robinson. I thought it was a foul by Ings. [Burnley] scored from the resultant free-kick. Paul remonstrated with the referee, who gave Paul a yellow card, but he mocked him about the score line at the time. This is totally unacceptable. I am not questioning his performance, but he knows what he said and it is not acceptable in any walk of life This was the only downside, and I have to flag it up. It is that it is not acceptable for an official to mock any player at any stage.'

Can you just imagine the relentless slanging that officials receive from 'real football men' like Clark and Robinson all game, every game? Frankly, you couldn't pay us enough to do their jobs most weeks.

The hypocrisy is super strength in this one.

Clark felt that the incident – which he said came as the Isle of Wight referee booked Robinson for dissent following the Clarets' second goal – took the gloss off a tremendous fight back by his side.

They trailed three times against second-placed Burnley to earn a valuable point with on-loan Federico Macheda scoring a last-minute equaliser, after which Clark was seen apparently kicking the advertising hoardings in celebration.

'I was furious and I lost my temper,' said the Birmingham boss. 'There seemed to be a bit of an arrogance among the officials and that is not being accepted. When my captain is fighting for the club and the supporters are backing my team and when I am working as hard as I can to get the results to remain in the league, getting mocked by an official is something I am not going to accept. I am not questioning his performance. But he knows what he said and it is not acceptable in any walk of life. Clark added: 'I will be wanting to take it further.'

BLACK CYCLING SHORTS

During a game between Watford and Walsall the referee asked Paul to remove his black cycling shorts. Paul thought the referee was out of order, telling him to change his shorts halfway through the game, and especially when Watford were defending. The only thing he could do was to get the shorts removed as quickly as possible, which is why he changed at the side of the pitch. Later in the game the fans may have seen him go down injured, only for him to get to his feet laughing just as physiotherapist Paul Rastrick reached him. Paul assures us that it wasn't deliberate time wasting because he did not see 'Razza' coming onto the pitch as he had his back to him, he was getting up and was messing around with Neil Cox which was why he was laughing. He genuinely was not thinking about time wasting although the referee and the Walsall fans took a different view.

UNWRITTEN RULES

As reported in *The Birmingham Mail*:

Paul Robinson has explained why he unwittingly almost caused a storm in Birmingham City's home defeat to Watford.

3 August 2013 Lost 0–1 Attendance: 18.830

And the Blues captain took a little dig at the Hornets players' tendency to 'roll about' after being challenged.

Robinson apologised for not following an unwritten football rule after the opposition side put the ball out of play in order for one of their players to receive treatment. The incident happened as Saturday's Championship season opener was reaching its climax. Watford substitute Cristian Battocchio went down and the ball was knocked off the field near the St Andrew's dug outs.

Robinson picked it up and promptly sent Lee Novak away down the left on the attack. He was one-on-one against Lloyd Doyley, who stopped him, and then squared up to the Blues striker. As the kerfuffle continued involving several players pushing and shoving, Gianfranco Zola was up in his technical area fuming and Lee Clark walked over to calm him down.

'I hold my hands up and apologise for that,' said Robinson, a former Watford favourite. 'They had kicked the ball out, the referee told their lad to get up, so as far as I knew, the referee just said to throw it. That's where the confusion came from. If the referee just said something to me, or the physiotherapist was going to come on, I would have thrown it back to them. I apologised to Zola straight after as I was just going off what the referee had indicated with his arm – to take the throw-in as normal.

"Then when he brought play back for a drop ball I kicked it back to them. This is what we have got to get sorted with referees and players. We have got to have this communication because if we had scored from it, what do you do? Their player was rolling around, the ball was kicked out, and he got straight back up. They were rolling around and rolling around (all game). The referee saw what was happening and played on a couple of times before. But it's that consistency. If players know what's going on then it will mean the game will flow a bit more.'

Clark said that had Blues scored from the throw-in he would have instructed his team to let Watford go down the other end from the re-start and score themselves.

Robinson said: 'Would he? I think sportsmanship has to come into the game. If the manager tells you to do that, then as players we do that, as part of respect.'

LOAN SYSTEM

I think the loan system is great for lower division teams, as it gives it a chance to get better quality players into their squads and enables those players the opportunity to play regular football. As we know 'loanees' do not always work out positively for the hosting club and this is often due to the lack of homework done by the management team.

Managers have a fantastically effective network, which enables them to find out about a player – what's his attitude (there's that word again!) like? Will he gel with the manager, the staff and the players?

The bottom line is that whatever a manager needs to know he can find out via the network. For example when Gary Rowett joined Birmingham City, before he had taken charge of a game, he had signed Michael Morrison on loan from Charlton Athletic. Why? Because he had done his homework – he knew Blues needed to strengthen defensively, he knew Michael was available, he knew he had the skills to sort out the weakness in the back four and he knew his personality and attitude was right for the club – because as an ex-Birmingham City player he knew the ethos of the club. It's all about getting the homework right!

9.

'Representative Honours'

Early in his Watford career Paul was asked the question:

'Do you ever have hopes of getting involved in the England squad?'

He replied: 'I am an ambitious person, and I would love to play for England and always would if I was given the opportunity. I will always be available for England until I stop playing. I will just keep trying my best and hope that the chance comes along. I play to high standards every week but it all comes down to one man giving me my chance and hopefully one day Mr Capello will give me that chance. We will just have to see and keep my fingers crossed.'

Well as we now know Mr Capello did not give Paul his chance at Full International but Paul did get to wear the colours of England on three occasions for the England Under-21 team and once for the Nationwide League Under-21 representative team.

Paul's England Under-21 appearances were part of the UEFA Under-21 European Championship tournament held between 1998 and 2000. In England's qualifying group were Sweden, Poland and Bulgaria and he has a cap and his number six shirt in his possession to remember those matches.

Paul was called into the squad to replace Matthew Upson of Arsenal. The squad announced was:

Ball (Everton), Barry (Aston Villa), Beattie (Southampton), Bowyer (Leeds), Bridges (Sunderland), Brown (Manchester United), Cresswell (York City), Carragher (Liverpool), Curtis (Manchester United), Euell

(Wimbledon), Greening (Manchester United), Hendrie (Aston Villa), Heskey (Leicester), Jansen (Blackburn Rovers), Johnson (Crewe), Lampard (West Ham United), Marshall (Norwich), Mills (Charlton Athletic), Mullins (Crystal Palace), O'Brien (Bradford), Paul Robinson (Leeds), Paul Robinson (Watford), Simonsen (Everton), Williams (Sunderland), Wright (Ipswich).

The details of the three games Robbo played are listed below.

England 3 Sweden 0 4 June 1999

Team: Richard Wright, Kieron Dyer, Paul Robinson (booked 83 minutes), Wes Brown, Danny Mills, Seth Johnson, Frank Lampard (booked 90 minutes), Jamie Garragher, Carl Cort, Richard Cresswell (Jonathan Greening 70 minutes), Curtis Woodhouse (Booked 53 minutes, John Curtis 56 minutes).
Substitutes unused: Gareth Barry, Ledley King, Hayden Mullins, Lee Morris.
Coach: Peter Taylor.

Sweden: Dime Jankulovski, Christoffer Andersson, Olof Mellberg (Captain), Kristoffer Arvhage, Erik Edman, Tobias Linderoth, Marcus Vaapil (Jeffrey Aubynn 76 minutes), Olof Persson, Bjorn Enqvist (Par Karlsson 65 minutes) Christian Lundstrom (Fredrik Berglund 65 minutes).
Substitutes unused: Ola Tidman, Mattias Kronvall, Filip Bergman and Andreas Nicklasson.
Coach: Thomas Lyth.

Attendance: 13,045 • **Referee:** Erol Ersoy (TURKEY). • **Venue:** The Alfred McAlpine Stadium, Huddersfield. • **Scorers:** Cort (29 and 79 minutes), Cresswell (44 minutes).

Paul recalls: 'I played on the left of a back three with Jamie Garragher and Wes Brown. You only got a cap when you played, so if you were an unused substitute then no cap!'

Bulgaria 0 England 1 8 June 1999

England: Steven Simonsen, John Curtis, Paul Robinson, Wes Brown, Hayden Mullins, Seth Johnson (booked 74 minutes), Jonathan Greening, Jamie Garragher (Captain), Carl Cort, Richard Cresswell (Lee Morris 72 minutes), Curtis Woodhouse.
Scorer: Cort (87 minutes).
Substitutes unused: Gareth Barry, Darren Holloway, Ledley King and Gary McSheffrey.
Coach: Peter Taylor.

Bulgaria: Yordan Gospodinov, Radoslav Komitov, Ivan Raitchev Ivanov, Krassimir Tchomakov, Zhivko Zhelev, Zahari Sirakov, Svetoslav Todorov (Stoyko Sakaliev 81 minutes), Angel Stolkov (Georgi Peev 46 minutes), Georgi Chilikov (Velizar Dimitrov 82 minutes), Marcho Dafchev (booked 30 minutes), Svetoslav Petrov.
Substitutes unused: Todor Kyuchukov, Stanislav Bachev, Dimitar Telkiyski.
Coach: Stoitcho Mladenov.

Referee: Sandor Piller (HUNGARY). • **Attendance:** 6,000
• **Venue:** Hristo Botev Stadiion, Gradski Vratsa.

Paul recalls: 'In this game I was given the duties of left wing-back and it was a miserable match. Afterwards we were taken to watch the senior game against Bulgaria where Kevin Phillips was playing.'

Poland 3 England 1 7 September 1999

England: Nicky Weaver, John Curtis (Yellow card 62 minutes, Curtis Woodhouse 66 minutes) Paul Robinson, Jamie Garragher (Captain), Danny Mills, Matthew Upson (Yellow card 61 minutes), Jonathan Greening (David Thompson 81 minutes) Steven Gerard, James Beattie, Carl Cort (Darius Vassell 46 minutes) Jody Morris.
Scorer: Mills 48 minutes.
Substitutes unused: Stuart Taylor, Michael Ball, Ledley King and Luke Young.
Coach: Howard Wilkinson.

Poland: Andrzej Bledzewski (Captain), Arkadiusz Glowacki, Maciej Terlecki, Marcin Baszczynski, Jaroslaw Bieniuk (Yellow card 89 minutes), Arkadiusz Radomski, Kamil Kosowski, Pawel Sobczak (Lukasx Sosin 89 minutes), Miroslav Spizak (Tomasz Dawidowski 56 minutes), Grzegorz Bonk (Tomasz Sokolowski 70 minutes), Lukasz Kubix .
Scorers: Kubik 46 minutes, Dawidowski 57 minutes, Sobczak 61 minutes.
Substitutes unused: Jakub Wierzchowski, Jacek Magiera, Maciej Scherfchen.
Coach: Pawel Janus.

Referee: Pascal Garibian (France). • **Attendance:** 1,500
• **Venue:** Stadion Orien, Plock.

England Under-21 Shirt

England Under-21 Cap

Paul was selected to be part of the Nationwide League's Under 21 team to play the Italian League on 28 November 1998 kick-off 2.30 at Stadio 1 Liberati. Terni. The score was 1–1. Scorer for the League was Luton Town's Sean Evers but the opposition equalised through a penalty.

Paul tells the story:

It was quite a shock for me when I found out I was in the squad. To be honest I didn't even know about the game. I found out a couple of weeks before the game. Kenny Jacket called me and Gifton Noel-Williams into the office and said we had been selected as part of the League's Under-21 squad to go to Italy with Peter Taylor. I didn't know what to say. I though he was messing around. The trip to Italy meant we had to meet up on the Sunday before the game. We flew out on the Monday, landed at Rome and it was about a 90-minute drive to the hotel, which was in the middle of nowhere. It was freezing out there. I was sharing a room with Gifton and it took us a while to get the heating working in our room. It was the first time in quite a while that I had travelled with a team other than Watford. I knew a couple of the lads but it wasn't a problem because by the end of the first day, I had spoken to most of the players. Some of the lads were quite forward and came up and spoke to you. When you train together, you soon get to know who's who. The match was played on a Wednesday afternoon and attracted a crowd in the hundreds rather than thousands. I think the police might have been expecting a few more because there were loads of them and they were wearing their riot hats. I was impressed with the standard of play; it was quick, certainly as quick as any First Division game here. The Italian forwards were sharp and always on the move. I thought it might be quicker than I was used to but I found I was able to cope with it okay. I started on the left of a three-man defence but eventually found myself in the middle. I had not played in the centre of defence before. I was comfortable with that.

It was certainly a good chance for me to learn. I was really pleased with the way I played and it was a great experience for me. Peter Taylor, the England Under-21 manager and former Hornets coach, took the team, so it was a chance to impress him. Alongside him was Glenn Roeder and Watford's goalkeeping coach Peter Bonetti, so the Vicarage Road connection was strong. Taylor had seen me play against Norwich and Oxford and Kenny Jackett said he was suitably impressed.

Noel-Williams picked up an ankle knock on Monday while training in Italy and the slight injury kept him on the bench but Robbo put in a good performance as a central defender in the 3-5-2 formation. Club life president of Watford and former vice-chairman Geoff Smith was in Italy watching the game and he reported, "Paul was excellent in what was not his normal position. I spoke with Glenn Roeder after the game and he couldn't praise Paul enough. He said he was a credit to Watford who got better and better as the game went on and is a real prospect."

Gifton commented on the game saying, 'Robbo has dug in hard like me. All the young players have … but Robbo and me have got a bit of acknowledgement.'

Italian Award

Paul was an unused substitute for the full England Squad in a European Championship 2002–2004 Group Seven qualification match in Turkey and has an England Pennant to remember the event.

Turkey 0 England 0

Turkey: RECBER Rustu (Yellow card 80 minutes), UZULMEZ Ibrahim, KORKMAZ Bulent, AKYEL Faith, OZALAN Alpay, BELOZOGLU Emre (PENBE Ergun 79 minutes), BURUK Okay (MANSIZ Ilhan 67 minutes), KERIMOGLU Tugay (Yellow card 62 minutes), SUKUR Hakan (Yellow card 58 minutes), KAHVECI Nihat, YALCIN A.R. Sergen (AZANLI Tuncay 61 minutes).
Unused Substitutes: Omer Catkic, Yildiray Basturk, Emre Asik, Umit Davala.

England: David James, Gary Neville, Ashley Cole, Steven Gerrard, John Terry, Sol Campbell, David Beckham (Captain – Missed Penalty 36 minutes), Paul Scholes (Frank Lampard 88 minutes), Wayne Rooney (Kieron Dyer 71 minutes), Emile Heskey (Darius Vassell 67 minutes), Nicky Butt (Yellow card 81 minutes)
Unused Substitutes: Phil Neville, Paul Robinson, Matt Upson, Wayne Bridge.
Coach: Sven-Goran Eriksson.

Attendance: 42,000 • **Referee:** Pierlugi Collina (Italy)
• **Venue:** Sukru Saracoglu Stadyuma, Kadikoy, Instanbul.

England Pennant

10.

'Match Day'

Birmingham 2 – Notts Forest 1 • Saturday 29 November 2014

What a match; a goal of the year contender from David Cotterill – an 'offside' equaliser – a deliberate hand ball preventing a goal thereby resulting in a penalty and a sending off – a substitute being booked as he warmed up on pitch side and it was Trevor Francis Day. More importantly Blues won again to continue our unbeaten run of five games since the appointment of Gary Rowett and Robbo was being 'shadowed' for this book!

Robbo was keen to give readers of his book an insight into what happens behind the scenes on a home match day so here goes:

We, Harry my photographer and I, arrived at The Century car park in Garrison Lane virtually opposite The Royal George public house on the corner of Tilton Road. This is the Press car park and having explained to the car park attendant that I do not work for a newspaper but am still entitled to park here, I park up – it's 12.15.

The Press Office which is located in the Main Stand opens at 12.30 and we are greeted by Lorraine who issues me with an 'Access All Areas' pass and Harry with a Press pass – 'you can keep the passes but can you return the lanyards before you leave?' This seems odd but this is Birmingham City Football Club!

It is of average size. The Press Office is no more than 12 feet square, but off it is an IT and a Radio Broadcast room with an exit in the far left-hand corner which leads onto the old tunnel beneath the stand. This was the tunnel, which was used when the teams entered on to the pitch at the halfway line.

The main room includes a reception desk where the members of the Press sign in, receive their passes and complimentary programme, alongside the right-hand wall is a table with coffee and tea flasks, which are refilled on numerous occasions throughout the day! The pre-printed menu announces available food as being 'savoury potato wedges and assorted sandwiches'. The room is set up for manager's post-match press interviews – in the far right-hand corner is the familiar club/sponsors backdrop which we see behind every manager interviewed on television, in front of that is the manager's table and chair with the press chairs set up in a semi-circle with about three rows.

Familiar faces include: Tom Ross from Free Radio 80, Bob Hall (ex-Central News), Colin Tattum and Joe Gallagher.

Joe Gallagher works part-time for the Press Association on match days, gathering statistics on the Blues games and is a familiar face at all home games, once he knows what I am doing there he gives me an instant appraisal of Robbo: 'I've never seen him pull out of a tackle, he's a motivator both on and off the pitch and must be great to play alongside – and he's a good bloke.' At the end of the game the Press Association statistics reveal that since his arrival at The Blues, Robbo has made 120 Clearances, 17 Blocks, Committed 21 Fouls, received four Yellow cards and no Red cards.

We drift out into the old tunnel and move down the new tunnel towards the dressing-room area beneath the Gil Merrick Stand, we are told by the security guys that my 'Access All Areas' pass only lives up to its name if it is enhanced by a green stick-on dot, which is already on Harry's Press pass.

I get my pass enhanced and we are offered seats in the Press Box to enable us to watch the match, although grateful for the offer we decline it, in the hope that once the match kicks off we can return to our season ticket seats in The Kop Stand.

At 12.44 we are pitch side looking at an empty stadium with only stewards receiving their briefings at various locations around the seating areas.

An empty St Andrew's

Players begin to arrive, Cotterill, Novak and Randolph being the first; Rita Greenway passes us on the way to meet with the manager in the Dressing Room area. I have known Rita since 1993 when she was manager's assistant to Terry Cooper – how many managers has she looked after?

In recent times under Lee Clark players were told to arrive at 12 o'clock so that they could breakfast together but after a sequence of poor results too long to document, Lee decided to stop the breakfast and get players to arrive around 13.00 hours, as he felt that the afternoon was too long and the players could have lost concentration by being bored by the time the day was over!

Robbo arrives dead on time for our rendezvous at 13.15 accompanied by his Mum and two youngest sons, Archie and Dexter. His Mom, Sandra has brought up from Watford a box full of scrapbooks she has kept on Paul's playing career for me to use as material for this book. Caroline is away with Luke watching him play Rugby and Paul's Dad, Mel is with Jamie who has training for the Blues Academy.

Robbo arrives at 13.15 hours

After numerous signings Robbo enters the stadium via the entrance to the left-hand side of the Main Stand Reception and walks pitch side down to the expanding white structure, which is the new tunnel towards the dressing room. His generous nature means he has a smile and time for everyone he encounters whether it be radio broadcasters such as Tom Ross or security and stewards.

Robbo in T.M.Lewin club suit

We are aware we are not allowed in the dressing room but we know Robbo's routine. It's 13.48 as he enters the dressing room corridor and heads for his pre-match massage, which he believes to be a crucial part of his match preparation.

Robbo down the tunnel to the dressing room

At 14.12 Kevin Poole newly appointed goalkeeping coach starts the warm up for Darren Randolph and Colin Doyle, which always happens at the Tilton Road Stand end using temporary goals to the left of the match goals presumably to protect the goal area.

At 14.20 Robbo leads out the squad for the pre-match warm up with Paul Caddis in close proximity.

Lined up and ready to go – Team Caddis versus Team Robbo

After a brief session knocking the balls around, the squad splits in to two lines one of which is led by Robbo the other by Caddis. Robbo takes his warm up very seriously and makes every effort to ensure he benefits from the various runs, which are keenly overseen by Tom Page, Head of Sports Science.

Also active as part of the warm up are Assistant Manager, Kevin Summerfield and First Team Coach Mark Sale both of which like Kevin Poole and Gary Rowett played for The Blues.

Warming Up – Callum Reilly, Robbo, Caddis
and Mark Sale hands in pocket

At 14.27 the squad forms a circle and completes a number of specifically designed stretches. Each player has their own preference regarding what they wear for the warm up session, varying from track suit bottoms to shorts, Shower-proof training tops to training shirts, Robbo prefers white shorts and training top.

It's 14.32 and its skills time: passing in rows of two – 13 minutes later the bibs are on for the starting eleven and we play 'keep the ball' after that depending on the player's position it's shooting or heading practice. At

14.45 the warm up is over and it is back to the dressing room for final preparation. For Paul this is superstitious routine: both shin pads have the name of his wife and four sons inscribed upon them, he always puts the left one on first, then he kisses his wedding ring before taking it off and putting in the same pocket of his suit. A blast from the smelling salts and he is ready to go!

At 14.51 the flag bearers are lined up outside the tunnel and *Mr Blue Sky* by The Electric Light Orchestra blasts from the Tannoy system. As always the atmosphere created by ELO is diminished when the *Keep Right On!* video is shown on the big screen with its monotone voiceover. It's match time and the teams parade on to the pitch lead by Trevor Francis hand in hand with his two grandsons acting as mascots.

It's Trevor Francis Day – he leads out the teams accompanied by his grandsons

Robbo leads out the team – Nottingham Forest goalkeeper,
Karl Darlow is Ken Leek's grandson

Ian Pugh, Stadium Manager escorted us pitch side in front of the Gil Merrick Stand to The Kop as we made our way to our seats in Section 24 Row 18.

The team reads: Randolph; Caddis, Morrison, Robinson, Grounds; Gleeson, Gray, Davis, Cotterill; Shinnie and Donaldson.

10 minutes – Goal for Blues – 'From the right Cotterill weaved his way infield and smacked a fizzing, rising effort that went just inside the far, top corner. St Andrew's went momentarily quiet, stunned at the quality of Cotterill's strike, before erupting into euphoria.' Brian Dick –*Sunday Mercury* 30/11/14

21 minutes into the game the crowd spontaneous stand up to applaud the anniversary of the Birmingham Pub Bombings.

15.48 Half-time whistle blows it's 1–0 and the place is buzzing. Robbo turns to the Tilton Road crowd and gestures to ask for the support to continue in the second half.

During the half-time interval the award-winning 'Chip and Win' is put to one side so that at 15.52 Trevor Francis could receive his 'Walk of Stars' star from the Lord Mayor of Birmingham, Councillor Shafique Shah and Jasper Carrott, the Chairman of the Walk of Stars committee. Trevor's Star will be placed on Broad Street along with those celebrating the success of Brummies and adopted-Brummies such as TF.

There was a poignant moment during the interval when the crowd was asked to given a standing ovation as the names of the victims of the Birmingham Pub bombings were read out from the Big Screen.

With Blues attacking the Tilton Road End, which has become a tradition in recent seasons (How lucky is Robbo with the toss of a coin?), the second half starts at 16.04.

At 62 minutes into the game a bizarre incident occurs: Three of the Forest substitutes are warming up pitch side when the ball goes out of play, one of the three substitutes delayed returning the ball to the field of play – I do not who it was and neither did referee Geoff Eltringham, but one of them was booked and I would suggest the player booked was not the miscreant. But it was either Tom Ince, Jamie Paterson, Dorus De Vries, Dexter Blackstock, Kelvin Wilson, Jack Hunt or Robert Tesche.

With six minutes to go of the 90, a goal for Forest from Britt Assombalonga 'In the 84th minute when Blues' thoughts turned to another home win Jamie Paterson flicked Eric Lichaj's cross into Assombalonga's path and the youngster headed coolly past Randolph,' Brian Dick *Sunday Mercury* 30/11/14. There was an immediate protest to the Assistant Referee from Caddis and Robbo that the goal was offside but their claims for justice were denied.

The Blues' claims for justice were upheld three minutes later when Michael Morrison's header from a David Cotterill corner was clearly handled on the line by Assombalonga. Clear that is to everyone other than the referee and his assistants. Eltringham awarded Blues a corner but everyone in the stadium knew it was a deliberate handball, including, fortunately for Blues, the Fourth Official, Nigel Smith communicated the right decision to the referee, who changed his decision. There were howls of protest from the Forest players but with Assombalonga heading for the dressing room, the ball was snatched up by Blues' penalty-taker Paul Caddis. (Paul had missed a penalty in the 0–8 defeat against Bournemouth only four matches ago and therefore showed immense confidence in wanting to take this one which based on the timing of incident was crucial for another Blues victory).

89 minutes – a goal for Blues from the penalty spot to put Blues back in the lead at 2–1. Caddis' success was all the more admirable based on the report from Brian Dick in the *Birmingham Mail* on Tuesday 2 December 2014 entitled, 'Caddis the winner in spot-kick mind games'. 'Blues match-winner Paul Caddis thanked the man who made his last-gasp penalty so comfortable – Nottingham Forest defender Jamaal Lascelles. "A lot happened in the five minutes from the decision to the penalty", Caddis revealed, "Lascelles kept chipping away in my ear. I would like to thank him because he told me the goalie always goes right. So I went the other side. Lascelles was just trying to put me off but I don't know why he was trying to delay it, as it had already been five minutes. He kept saying I will miss – and we would lose the game. But thanks very much".

Six minutes of additional time was indicated by the Fourth Official and no one was going to argue with that decision and at 16.56 the final whistle sounded.

Win, lose or draw Robbo always rallies the players to applaud the fans and on this occasion the applause was mutual.

We made our way back to the Press Office and were able to listen to Gary Rowett's post match interview, as did Stuart Pearce for the last five minutes which according to Joe Gallagher is very unusual as the away manager normally waits until the home manager has finished.

Gary Rowett After Match Press Conference

In the old tunnel with Clayton Donaldson in the background

At 17.15 we re-connected with Robbo in the old tunnel and went up into the Player's Lounge where Paul's family were waiting, having been joined by Mel and Jamie.

After a brief chat it was down the steps of the Main Stand Reception to be greeted by fans and well wishers and as usual Paul never refused a photograph or a signature.

Celebrating with the fans!
By 18.00 it was time to go – What a Day!

11.

'Captain's Log'

Tell the readers about your current Birmingham teammates:

Who is the best trainer?
ME, OBVIOUSLY
Note: before you condemn him for being 'big headed' – In The Official Blues Annual 2014 in the BACK CHAT section: MATT GREEN – DARREN RANDOLPH – CHRIS BURKE --CALLUM REILLY-SCOTT ALLAN and WILL PACKWOOD all nominated Paul as The Best Trainer.

Who has the worst dress sense?
ANDREW SHINNIE

Who is the best dancer?
I WILL TELL YOU AFTER THE CHRISTMAS PARTY 2014 – MITCH HANCOX

Who spends longest in front of the mirror?
OLLY LEE

Who is the joker in the dressing room?
PAUL CADDIS

Tell the readers about your FAVOURITES:

Who is your favourite Actor?
JASON STATHAM

Who is your favourite Actress?
SANDRA BULLOCK

What is your favourite Movie?
GLADIATOR

Who is your favourite Musician or Band?
ED SHEERAN and SAM SMITH

Where is your favourite Place?
PORTUGAL

What are your Pet Hates?
I'VE GOT A FEW:
LOSING
MESS – I AM A BIT O.C.D SO I LIKE
THINGS TO BE TIDY
BEING LATE FOR ANYTHING

If you were a character in any movie, who would it be?
IT WOULD HAVE TO BE JASON STATHAM IN TRANSPORTER

What do you do on your days off?
SPEND TIME WITH MY FAMILY AND PLAY GOLF.

Last Album Downloaded?
U2 BECAUSE IT WAS FREE ON ITUNES (October 2014)

Last Film Seen?
NIGHT AT THE MUSEUM 3 (The joy of having young children)

Describe yourself in three words?
PASSIONATE, WINNER, DETERMINED

What do you feel is your best attribute as a footballer?
MY DRIVE TO BE BETTER EACH DAY

The Best game of your career?
WATFORD BEATING LIVERPOOL AT ANFIELD 1–0 (SEE MEM-
ORABLE GAME 5)

Favourite goal you have scored?
HEADER AGAINST VILLA FOR THE ALBION
(SEE MEMORABLE GAME 7)

Favourite Away Ground?
THE EMIRATES

Tell the readers about your CHOICES:

Snow or Sun?
SUN

Twitter or Facebook?
TWITTER
On 15/01/2015 Robbo tweets: 7 points off play-offs! Come on the boys.
Great atmosphere again at St Andrew's and upwards we go #KRO"
P.R.@Robbo04pr

Coffee or Tea?
COFFEE

Beer or Lager?
LAGER

Chinese or Indian?
BOTH

Sweet or Savoury?
SWEET

Night In or Night Out?
NIGHT IN

Early Bird or Night Owl?
EARLY BIRD

Action or Comedy?
ACTION

Apple or Blackberry? (Not the fruit!)
APPLE

Sausage or Bacon?
BACON

Cats or Dogs?
DOGS

Bond or Bourne?
BOURNE

X Factor or Strictly Come Dancing?
X FACTOR

Tennis or Golf?
GOLF

*Coronation Street **or** East Enders?*
NEITHER

Any Claims to Fame not covered elsewhere in the book?

Although it is included in the book as a venue for Memorable Games – for any footballer playing at Wembley has a claim to fame. 'I can't imagine what it must feel like to be a professional footballer and to never have played under the Twin Towers, having said that the history books show that many famous players did not grace the home of football during their playing days. The building of the New Wembley stadium brought about a new era for English football and the stadium itself is superb. I am a lucky man though in that I have had the opportunity to play at both Wembley's and that will always stay with me throughout my life – my claim to fame!

What would you do for a career if you weren't a footballer?

I honestly don't know! I mean I love my sport. I love playing golf so whether I would have taken that a little more seriously when I was at a young age. It was just a bit of fun at the time, I always dedicated myself to football and that's all I've wanted to do.

Who is your sporting hero?

MUHAMMAD ALI FOR HIS PROFESSIONALISM AND SEVE BALLESTEROS

What would you be if you weren't a sportsman?

SERIOUSLY I DON'T KNOW

Which other sportsman would you like to be?

RORY MCILROY OR SERGIO GARCIA – AN ENTERTAINING GOLFER

Career highlight?

TWO 'GREAT ESCAPES' (SEE MEMORABLE GAMES 8 AND 15)

... And the worst moment? LOSING 5–0 WHILST AT BOLTON AND

LOSING 8–0 WHILST AT THE BLUES (SEE MEMORABLE GAMES 12 AND 16)

If your house was burning down, what one possession would you save?
MY FAMILY FOLLOWED BY OUR DOG TIGGY

What's the best advice you've ever been given?
BELIEVE IN YOURSELF AND EXHIBIT MENTAL STRENGTH – I GOT THAT FROM GRAHAM TAYLOR WHILST AT WATFORD

Favourite karaoke song?
ICE ICE BABY – VANILLA ICE

Most-listened to artist on your phone, tablet and laptop?
SAM SMITH and ED SHEERAN

Last book you read?
WATT NICHOLLS' LATEST

Favourite pre-match meal?
POACHED EGGS ON TOAST

Can you cook and what is your Signature dish?
YES, SPAGHETTI BOLOGNESE AND I ALSO ENJOY BAKING

In a film of your life, who would you like to play you?
JASON STATHAM

What's the most expensive thing you've ever bought?
FORD MUSTANG – BUT I HAD TO LET IT GO BECAUSE IN CERTAIN CONDITIONS IT WAS DANGEROUS!

In the BLUES News official match day programme for the match against Blackburn Rovers on 21 April 2014 there was an article entitled 'MY A TO Z WITH PAUL ROBINSON.'

Blues skipper Paul Robinson tackles a series of irreverent questions based around 26 topics of the alphabet. If you want to know which film he is happy to watch time and again, which soccer pundit he puts on mute or the one football memento he treasures most the turn overleaf and all will be revealed ...

A IS FOR ADVICE

What advice would you give any budding young footballers?
JUST ENJOY THE GAME AND LOVE PLAYING FOOTBALL AND MAKE THE MOST OF IT WHILE YOU CAN. IT'S A FANTASTIC SPORT TO BE INVOLVED IN.

B IS FOR BOX

What is your favourite TV programme?
I'VE GOT A FEW, BUT AT THE MOMENT I'M WATCHING HANNIBAL AND THE FOLLOWING. IT'S OUT OF THOSE TWO BECAUSE THEY'RE BOTH VERY GOOD.

C IS FOR COMRADES

Who are your best friends in football?
MY CLOSEST FRIENDS IN FOOTBALL ARE JONATHAN GREENING AND KEVIN PHILLIPS.

D IS FOR DULL

Is there a football pundit on radio or TV that you find really tedious?
MICHAEL OWEN ON BT SPORT. I HAVE TO PUSH MUTE WHEN I'M LISTENING TO IT! HE WAS A GOOD FOOTBALLER, BUT NOT SO GOOD AS A PUNDIT.

E IS FOR EXPERIENCE

What is the most important lesson life has taught you?

JUST TO MAKE THE MOST OF EVERY OPPORTUNITY THAT IS GIVEN TO YOU AND NOT TO THROW IT AWAY. IF THERE IS AN OPPORTUNITY THERE, JUST GRAB IT WITH BOTH HANDS.

F IS FOR FLICKS

What's your favourite film of all-time?

DEFINITELY GLADIATOR. I LOVE WATCHING THAT FILM AND COULD WATCH IT ALL THE TIME.

G IS FOR GLOBE

Is there anywhere in the world that you'd like to retire to?

NOT REALLY, BUT I'D LOVE TO SEE MORE OF THE WORLD WHEN I RETIRE BECAUSE YOU HAVE MORE TIME TO DO THAT. I'D LOVE TO GO TO LAS VEGAS WITH MY WIFE, BUT WE WANT TO SAVE IT FOR A SPECIAL TIME.

H IS FOR HEADLINE

What would be your dream newspaper headline?

ROBINSON IS NEW ENGLAND MANAGER.

I IS FOR INSTRUMENT

Can you play a musical instrument?

NO I'M RUBBISH, ALTHOUGH I ALWAYS WANTED TO LEARN THE PIANO OR GUITAR. BOTH OF MY ELDEST SONS PLAY THE GUITAR AND IT'S BRILLIANT LISTENING TO THEM AND HOW THEY CAN READ MUSIC AT SUCH A YOUNG AGE.

J IS FOR JUDGE

If you could choose to be a judge on any of the TV talent shows, which one would it be?

PROBABLY X-FACTOR BECAUSE IT SEEMS A BIT OF A LAUGH AND A JOKE. I THINK EVEN THOUGH I KNOW NOTHING ABOUT MUSIC I'D BE MR NICE!

K IS FOR KID

What's your favourite memory from childhood?

GOING ON HOLIDAY WITH MY FAMILY. WHEN YOU'RE LITTLE IT'S GREAT TO GO TO DIFFERENT PLACES AWAY FROM YOUR OWN COUNTRY. I THINK THE FIRST ONE WE WENT ON WAS SPAIN, WHICH WAS LOVELY.

L IS FOR LUMINARY

Which footballer did you idolise when you were younger?

WHEN I WAS A KID I WAS A BIG TOTTENHAM FAN, SO I USED TO IDOLISE PAUL GASCOIGNE. WHEN I WAS A LEFT-BACK IT WOULD HAVE BEEN PAOLO MALDINI OR STUART PEARCE.

M IS FOR MEMENTO

What's the one football memento that you'll never give away?

I WOULDN'T GIVE ANY OF MY MEMENTOES AWAY BECAUSE THEY'RE ALL PRECIOUS AND WHAT I'VE EARNED THROUGH MY CAREER. THE ONE ITEM THAT IS PARTICULARLY PRECIOUS IS THE WINNERS' MEDAL I GOT WHEN WE WON THE CHAMPIONSHIP WITH WEST BROM.

N IS FOR NET-BUSTER

What's the best goal you've ever scored and talk us through it?

DEFINITELY MY HEADER AGAINST ASTON VILLA FOR WEST BROM. RICCARDO SCIMECA PROVIDED THE CROSS FOR ME AND I JUST POPPED UP BACK STICK AND HEADED IT IN. IT WAS A LAST MINUTE EQUALISER AT VILLA PARK.

O IS FOR OBJECT

What is the one household object you couldn't live without?

DEFINITELY MY TV. I LIKE WATCHING TV.

P IS FOR PRE-MATCH

What is your normal pre-match meal?

NORMALLY IT'S A BOILED EGG ON TOAST.

Q IS FOR QUIZ

If you were taking part in a pub quiz, what would be your best topic be?

FILMS

R IS FOR RETIREMENT

When you retire from playing football, what would you like to do?

I'D LIKE TO WORK MY WAY UP THE LADDER AND GO INTO COACHING OR MANAGEMENT EVENTUALLY. I'VE ALREADY PASSED MY UEFA LEVEL B COACHING BADGE. I JUST NEED TO GET MY A NOW. THAT WILL PROBABLY TAKE JUST OVER A YEAR TO DO.

S IS FOR SIGNATURE

Can you remember your first autograph, both given and received?

THE FIRST ONE I GAVE WAS WHEN I WAS AT WATFORD AND HAD JUST COME THROUGH THE RANKS. RECEIVED, IT WOULD BE WHEN I GOT A SIGNED SHIRT FOR MY BOYS OFF JOHN TERRY.

T IS FOR TRANSPORT

When was the last time you used public transport?

I GOT THE TRAIN DOWN TO LONDON AT CHRISTMAS.

U IS FOR UNRIVALLED

Who is the best player you have ever seen in your position?

PAOLO MALDINI OR ASHLEY COLE.

V IS FOR VOCIFEROUS

Who is the loudest manager that you've played under?

IT'S GOT TO BE GARY MEGSON, BECAUSE HE CONTINUOUSLY SHOUTS AT YOU.

W IS FOR WHILE AWAY THE TIME

When you're travelling to away games on the team coach, what do you do to stop yourself getting bored?

I JUST CATCH UP ON FILMS ON MY IPAD, LISTEN TO A BIT OF MUSIC OR HAVE A BIT OF BANTER WITH THE LADS.

X IS FOR EXHILARATING

What's the most memorable match you've played in?

IT'S GOT TO BE THE GREAT ESCAPE WITH WEST BROM. TO STAY UP IN THE LAST GAME WE HAD TO WIN AT HOME AGAINST PORTSMOUTH AND WE WON 2–0.

Y IS FOR YUMMY

What's the food you love but you know it's not good for you?

I LIKE A BURGER AS A TREAT EVERY NOW AND AGAIN, BUT I KNOW THEY'RE NOT GOOD FOR YOU!

Z IS FOR ZENITH

On average, how many hours sleep do you normally get in a night?

WITH MY KIDS ROUGHLY SIX! I'M TIRED BUT I GET THROUGH THE DAY WITH THAT.

Epilogue

TIMELINE

Season	Date	Moving From	Moving To	Market Value	Transfer Fee
1996–97	01/07/96	FC Watford U18	Watford	–	–
2003–04	01/09/03	Watford	West Bromwich Albion	–	£330,000
2009–10	01/08/09	West Bromwich Albion	Bolton Wanderers	£2,020,000	Loan
2009–10	01/12/09	Bolton Wanderers	West Bromwich Albion	£2,020,000	End of Loan
2009–10	01/01/10	West Bromwich Albion	Bolton Wanderers	£2,020,000	£1,060,000
2011–12	06/03/12	Bolton Wanderers	Leeds United	£1,320,000	Loan
2011–12	01/05/12	Leeds United	Bolton Wanderers	£1,320,000	End of Loan
2012–13	01/07/12	Bolton Wanderers	Unemployed	£440,000	
2012–13	25/09/12	Unemployed	Birmingham City	£440,000	
2013–14					Current Value £220,000 at 8/01/2014
2014–15	Contracted to 30/06/15				

OFF THE FIELD INTERESTS

HIV TESTING SAVES LIVES

In November 2014 West Midland football clubs decided to create an awareness campaign – to coincide with National HIV testing Week 22 to 29 November.

As well as Paul, representing Birmingham City, Ron Vlaar of Aston Villa, Sam Ricketts of Wolverhampton Wanderers and Christ Brunt of West Bromwich Albion were also part of the campaign, which had as it's strapline – 'You can live a long happy life with HIV if you get tested.'

MOLLY OLLY

The Lion, the Ride and the Robinsons

Paul, Caroline and members of the Molly Olly Team visited the Ward 15 (Oncology Ward) and the Teenage Cancer Unit to give out Olly the Brave to all the children. The children loved meeting a celebrity and it was a real privilege for us all to meet the remarkable children and their families. Our big Olly kept Paul and Caroline company and everyone (even some Aston Villa fans!) loved meeting them both. Having a seven foot lion on the ward certainly brightened up the day for everyone and over 50 Olly's have been donated to different departments around the hospital.

So the following day the Robinsons started their own challenge to help raise awareness of Olly. How? A cycle challenge 125 miles in 24 hours. The journey began from Molly's school, Claverdon Primary on Tuesday lunchtime and ended at Paul's old senior school in Watford, St Michael's.

Neither of them are cyclists, but they trained hard so that their challenge would help make a difference.

They had a tremendous send off in Claverdon that was supported by JD and Roisin from Free Radio and all the children and teachers came out with banners and cheers to send them on their way. En route they stopped at Warwick, Stratford, Banbury, Oxford, Amersham, Rickmansworth and Watford and finished when they were welcomed in to St Michael's with a guard of honour. It was a great to arrive with such a fanfare and St

Michael's also proudly presented the charity with a cheque from their own fundraising initiatives.

Caroline tweeted … 'What an awful hill!!! Oh my days, but this challenge will be finished today, yet the children carry on with their battles tomorrow and that's what is so motivating.'

Paul wrote, 'Caroline and I have been truly inspired since meeting Rachel, Tim, Ben and Maeve Ollerenshaw in 2012 and we are so proud to be their friends. They are a beautiful family who have tragically gone through the devastation of losing their daughter/sister Molly to cancer in June 2011. Molly Olly's Wishes is their charity and they grant wishes for children with life limiting and terminal illnesses nationwide.'

The event was a great success and the charity reported, 'We received fantastic support and the amazing achievements of Paul and Caroline Robinson on their first major bike ride. It really was a great challenge and Molly Olly's would like to thank Paul and Caroline, Claverdon Primary, St Michael's School and everyone who came out to support.' Thank you to our sponsors:

- Studio Spicer Architects
- Go for Goals
- Premier Sports Solutions
- Heritage Leisure
- Abacus Chiropractic Clinic
- Burnt Tree Vehicle Hire for providing the Dream Bus for three days

And also a big thank you to everyone who came out to support them on their journey:

Merchants Wine Bar – Warwick – Warwick Sports Shop – Matthew Curtis Hair Salon and Jimbobs

Appendices

Team	Debut	Appearances (+ substitutes)	Goals	Yellows	Reds
Birmingham City	29 September 2012	104(5) (as at 23/01/15)	1	15	1
Leeds United	11 March 2012	9(1)	0	3	0
Bolton Wanderers	15 August 2009	81(6)	0	21	0
West Brom Albion	18 October 2003	235(3)	5	43	4
Watford	12 August 2000	248(0)	9	39	2
TOTAL		675(15)	15	121	7

Career History by season

Season	Club	Division	Appearances	Goals
1996–97	Watford	Division 2	17	0
1997–98	Watford	Division 2	25	2
1998–99	Watford	Division 1	34	0
1999–20	Watford	Premiership	32	0
2000–01	Watford	Division 1	44	0
2001–02	Watford	Division 1	43	4
2002–03	Watford	Division 1	42	3
2003–04	Watford	Division 1	11	0
	W.B.A.	Division 1	32	0
2004–05	W.B.A.	Premier	33	1
2005–06	W.B.A.	Premier	36	0
2006–07	W.B.A.	Championship	52	2
2007–08	W.B.A.	Championship	48	1
2008–09	W.B.A.	Premier	37	1
2009–10	Bolton	Premier	27	0
2010–11	Bolton	Premier	40	0
2011–12	Leeds	Championship	10	0
	Bolton	Premier	20	0
2012–13	Birmingham	Championship	37	0
2013–14	Birmingham	Championship	46	1
2014–15	Birmingham	Championship	23(3) AS AT 22/01/15	0

Medals:

Division 2 Champions Medal 1997–98 – Watford

Championship Winners medal – West Bromwich Albion

The Final Word

Reflections of Keith

Little did I know when my Dad, Eric took me to my first game at St Andrew's that it was the start of a 'love affair' with Birmingham City Football Club that has lasted 60 years.

As an eight-year-old who had been raised in Holmwood Road, Small Heath it was a short ride on my dad's shoulders up Green Lane to the Coventry Road and then into Cattell Lane to the turnstiles.

I went over the turnstiles whilst my Dad paid for his entrance and gave the operator 'a drink.'

My Dad was a barber – a 'short back and sides' expert and he was one of the first hairdressers in Sheldon to go 'mobile'. With his clippers and scissors on the back of his moped he did the 'rounds', which included memorably a few of the Blues players who lived in club houses on the Cranes Park Road estate.

Early 50s in design, the houses were semi-detached with bow windows up and down. Occasionally I went with him and on one such occasion we went to a house in Shepherd Road, which was occupied by Mr and Mrs Boyd.

It was April 1956 and I remember Mr Boyd walked funny due as I now understand to the fact that he was wearing a back brace. My Dad asked him if he would be playing to which Mrs Boyd replied 'Of course, he is can you see him not playing!' As an eight-year-old I was unaware of sarcasm particularly in a matrimonial context and therefore just accepted the fact that Len Boyd would be captaining Birmingham City in the FA Cup Final at Wembley sporting one of Dad's haircuts.

And that was the last contact I had with a current Birmingham City captain until July 2014 when I met Paul Robinson.

I recall my Dad telling me that Len would definitely play at Wembley because he had a 'never-say-die' approach to the game. He was a fierce competitor and always wanted to gain an advantage for his team at all times, he was very vocal and rallied the troops when required. He did not allow any player not to give 100% but was friendly and helpful to those who needed it. If a tackle needed to be made or a ball blocked, Boyd was always there – proud to wear the Royal Blue of Birmingham City Football Club.

He was a fan's favourite and would always sign an autograph either at the ground or at the training facility in Damson Lane, Sheldon. No E-bay or Gum Tree in those days – so every autograph was for the collector's sole benefit – just one signature in an autograph book or in a *Charles Buchan's Football Monthly* signed to the individual and a memory forever!

Sound familiar? Of course it does become even in the 1950s Birmingham City had an *UNSUNG HERO*.